How to
Get Started
in Export

THE SUNDAY TIMES

How to Get Started in Export

John Westwood

KoganPage

LONDON PHILADELPHIA NEW DELHI

Publisher's note
Every possible effort has been made to ensure that the information contained in this book is accurate at the time of going to press, and the publishers and author cannot accept responsibility for any errors or omissions, however caused. No responsibility for loss or damage occasioned to any person acting, or refraining from action, as a result of the material in this publication can be accepted by the editor, the publisher or the author.

First published in Great Britain and the United States in 2012 by Kogan Page Limited

120 Pentonville Road	1518 Walnut Street, Suite 1100	4737/23 Ansari Road
London N1 9JN	Philadelphia PA 19102	Daryaganj
United Kingdom	USA	New Delhi 110002
www.koganpage.com		India

© John Westwood, 2012

The right of John Westwood to be identified as the author of this work has been asserted by him in accordance with the Copyright, Designs and Patents Act 1988.

ISBN   978 0 7494 6371 7
E-ISBN   978 0 7494 6372 4

The views expressed in this book are those of the author, and are not necessarily the same as those of Times Newspapers Ltd.

British Library Cataloguing-in-Publication Data

A CIP record for this book is available from the British Library.

Library of Congress Cataloging-in-Publication Data

Westwood, John, 1947-
    How to get started in export / John Westwood. – 1st ed.
        p. cm.
    ISBN 978-0-7494-6371-7 – ISBN 978-0-7494-6372-4   1. Exports.
2. Marketing–Planning–Handbooks, manuals, etc.   I. Title.
    HF1414.4.W47 2012
    658.8'4–dc23
                                                    2011048478

Typeset by Graphicraft Limited, Hong Kong
Printed and bound in India by Replika Press Pvt Ltd

Contents

Introduction

Any company with a good product that it is successfully selling in its domestic market should think about starting to develop an export business. Exporting is not just for large companies and major multinationals – the majority of exporters in most countries are small businesses. Exporting really is a fantastic way to grow your business.

There has never been a better time for companies to move into exporting. All countries want to persuade more of their companies to export their products, and most governments provide assistance for their exporters.

There is a huge amount of information and assistance available to exporters, much of it on the internet. Even if your own government does not provide large amounts of support material for exporters on its own websites, you can still access free information on government websites in many other countries.

Hopefully the information in this book will guide you in the right direction to start your journey into exporting. Always take appropriate advice as you develop your export business, and where you need financial or legal advice make sure that you consult experts in those fields.

I have tried to make as much as possible of the material in this book applicable to exporting worldwide, regardless of the country that you are based in. Most material is truly global, but much is used globally and applied locally.

If you are new to exporting, this book will get you started on your export journey. But we hope that experienced exporters will also find much to help them develop and grow their businesses. Exporting is a team effort and will only succeed with the professional dedication of all of the members of your export team.

1

Why should companies export?

In recent years world trade has grown at a faster rate than world output. World exports of merchandise and commercial services are about $18.5 trillion. Merchandise exports in the form of manufactured goods, minerals and agricultural commodities now account for about 80 per cent of global trade, with services comprising the other 20 per cent. The proportion made up of services is continuing to increase year on year.

Why start exporting?

Any company that has good products and a steady level of business in its domestic market should logically consider exporting as a way of growing its business still further. The risks are higher, but the rewards can also be greater.

If your company has been successfully selling its products in its domestic market, there is a good chance that it will also be successful in overseas markets – at least in those where similar needs and conditions exist. Selling overseas may be more difficult, but at least you are selling something that you know you have sold successfully at home. So why should exporting be the top of your list of strategies to adopt? There are two very good reasons:

- **Exporting expands your available market.**
- **No other business activity receives so much encouragement and support.**

The potential market

According to the International Monetary Fund (IMF), the size of the world economy in 2011 was about $68 trillion. For any company anywhere in the world, the potential export market for its product is much larger than its potential domestic market. According to the US Small Business Administration, nearly 96 per cent of consumers live outside the United States, and even for a US company two-thirds of the world's purchasing power is in foreign countries.

The benefits of exporting

Exporting can help you to increase your potential market, increase your turnover, improve your business's reputation, avoid being over dependent on your domestic sales and provide a buffer to any cyclical deterioration in your domestic economy. Exporting companies can utilise their capacity more efficiently and gain economies of scale. By finding export markets in different hemispheres, agricultural suppliers can even out seasonal fluctuations in the demand for their products.

According to UK Trade & Investment (UKTI), **www.ukti.gov.uk**, companies that export:

- **improve their productivity;**
- **achieve levels of growth not possible domestically;**
- **increase the resilience of their revenues and profits;**
- **achieve economies of scale not possible domestically;**
- **increase the commercial lifespan of their products and services;**
- **increase the returns on their investment in R&D;**
- **improve their financial performance;**
- **feel the benefit.**

Academic research confirms that exporting companies are more productive than non-exporters, achieve stronger financial performance and are more likely to stay in business.

Doing business overseas gives companies increased exposure to new ideas. By working with international clients and partners, companies gain knowledge of different cultural environments and get a better insight into customers' requirements. They gain exposure to new technologies and ideas and also experience a wider range of competitors. This gives them the opportunity to develop new and improved products and services, which can help them to gain and retain competitiveness at home as well as overseas.

Government support for exporters

Trade is the lifeblood of economic growth so all governments do their best to promote both exporting and inward investment. It can be a difficult sell, though, and that is why many governments have organisations that provide advice, support and in many cases even financial assistance to companies that export. Twenty years ago only large exporting countries, mainly in the developed world, had government agencies to support their exporters. Nowadays almost every country, large or small, provides government support to its exporters. It is very likely that your country will have a government agency supporting export trade and inward investment. Virtually all governments provide vast amounts of information, advice to individual companies and even financial support for things such as market research, trade fairs and trade missions. Why do they do this?

They do it because they know that if they want to grow their economies, then part of this growth has to come from exports. This is particularly true for the established economies of the developed world. It is also becoming increasingly the case for developing countries. The increased growth rates over the last decade in countries in regions such as Africa and South America have been, in large part, fuelled by the growth in their exports of minerals and other commodities. See what official sources in some countries say themselves:

- **Exports account for nearly 30 per cent of UK GDP and contribute 60 per cent of UK productivity growth. One in four jobs in the UK** is linked to business overseas and up to 3.5 million UK jobs are linked both directly and indirectly to the country's trade with the EU (UKTI 2010).

- Exports accounted for nearly 25 per cent of US economic growth during the past decade and they are expected to grow by nearly 10 per cent per year for the next several years (US Department of Commerce 2008).
- It is estimated that exports provide more than 20 per cent of Australia's gross national income and that more than 1.7 million jobs nationally are dependent on the export sector (Austrade 2011).

But according to UK Trade & Investment (UKTI), even though the UK is a major exporting country, just one in 25 UK companies currently exports goods or services.

Government support organisations

Some of the best and most comprehensive government support organisations for exporters are those provided in the UK, the United States and Australia.

UK Trade & Investment (UKTI), **www.ukti.gov.uk**, was established by the government to assist UK exporters. UKTI has developed a national export strategy that for the first time consolidates all government support for exporters under one organisation, integrating the activities of the Department of Trade and Industry, the Foreign and Commonwealth Office, overseas embassies and regional and local providers of export services in the UK, including new arrangements with the Chambers of Commerce.

The US Department of Commerce and International Trade provides government support to US exporters. The US Commercial Service is the trade promotion arm of the Department of Commerce's International Trade Administration. It uses the US government's export portal, **www.export.gov**, as its main online resource for US exporters for market research, trade events, trade leads and information on how to export. Services offered include market intelligence, trade counselling, business matchmaking and trade advocacy.

The Australia Trade Commission (Austrade), **www.austrade.gov.au**, provides support to Australian exporters.

To show how extensive and helpful the support from these government organisations can be, the appendix on page 142 provides a summary of the services available to UK exporters from UKTI. Similar and equivalent types of support are available to exporters in many countries from their local government support agencies, so this really is an essential aspect to investigate.

Is your company ready to start exporting?

Developing new export markets takes time and money. There are many new challenges – from identifying the best markets and potential customers to making sure your product complies with local standards and regulations. Exporting isn't just an add-on to your existing business; it should be part of your overall business development strategy.

In developing your business, you may have concluded that you need to increase the volume of sales of particular products to make them more viable. If you already have a reasonable level of sales of these products in your domestic market, it is unlikely that you could achieve a 100 per cent increase in sales in your domestic market alone. But such an increase in sales may well be possible in markets where you are currently not selling: that is, overseas.

But you can't just say: 'OK that seems a good idea. Let's do it!' Before you start exporting you need to carry out an export audit, develop an export strategy and prepare a complete export plan, which includes looking at all the costs and risks involved. (We will look at export audits in Chapter 2 and show you how to develop an export strategy and prepare an export plan in Chapter 4.)

Potential risks involved in exporting are summarised below.

Greater complexity

- **Exporting involves all the usual marketing challenges. You have to find customers and persuade them to buy from you. You have to research the market so that you understand what the customers** want and how the market operates – both may be different from what you have found in your domestic market.

- You will need to cope with extra logistical problems, paperwork and contractual issues. You will probably need to get standard contracts prepared for selling directly, through agents and through distributors.
- You will need to comply with regulations in both your domestic and overseas markets, and these may not be the same.
- The protection of intellectual property can be difficult and more complex in overseas markets, and in some it may not be 100 per cent effective.

Increased pressure on your resources

- You will need additional resources, both in terms of skilled personnel and financing. Your personnel will need to possess or learn the skills required in dealing with export markets.
- Exporting may impact on your company's domestic activities. It may reveal capacity and productivity constraints.

Increased financial exposure

- Exporting will initially involve expenditure, which may impact on your company's cash flow.
- Payment terms will usually be longer than for domestic sales.
- There could be export financing and/or currency issues, and the additional risk of potential non-payment for goods and services supplied to overseas customers.
- At the same time you may have to meet extra costs for transport and insurance.

Dealing with these issues means additional costs for your business. Equally importantly, you may find that you just can't compete with local suppliers in some overseas markets. If the market only offers low margins or you don't have the extra resources that you need, you may decide that exporting is not for you. But if you have good products and efficient manufacturing, there will certainly be opportunities for you in overseas markets.

The extra costs of exporting

To support an export operation your company will need to train existing staff and add additional personnel with new skills. As existing personnel start to support your export business, they will no longer have the time to handle all their original responsibilities. So whether you train up existing staff or recruit new people for your export operations, you will still have additional personnel costs. Even a small ongoing export operation will require a minimum of one dedicated internal salesperson and one outside salesperson. You also have to add in travelling costs and other expenses.

That is the investment that you can easily see. But then you need to consider the fact that you may not be able to make the same level of margins in your export business as you do on your domestic sales. You have to be sure that your top management accept this and that they recognise that your export sales are additional sales and may need to be viewed as marginal business.

The exchange rate factor

Exporting is a continually changing ball game, and one of the main change factors that is completely outside your control is the movement of currency exchange rates. When you put together your budget for domestic sales for next year, in addition to sales and margins you will also include a number of assumptions, such as the estimated inflation rate, the rate of economic growth and the rate of value added tax. If you put together a budget for export sales, you also need to include assumptions for key exchange rates. You can reduce exchange rate risks by taking out forward exchange contracts (for a year or even up to two years ahead) to cover some of your export business. But what you cannot do is cover for the wider medium-term movements in exchange rates that often occur.

Getting top management on your side

If you have decided that selling your products overseas is a good expansion policy for your company and that the time is right to start now, you need to prepare justifications and make sure that top management, both in your own company and at head office (if you are part of a larger group), are behind you. Depending on the culture in your company you may only need to prepare a simple export plan that includes details of the opportunities, costs and risks, or you may need to prepare a complete marketing plan for your export venture, including a partial profit-and-loss account for the additional sales. A common problem in many companies is that although management accept a plan, they will suggest that you try to grow the sales first and then invest in the extra people to support the new business afterwards. This will not work with export sales. If you want to expand your overseas business you just cannot afford to be under-resourced.

How to get started

In exporting size is no obstacle. Small companies or even sole traders can expand their business by exporting, just as easily as large organisations. The spread of company size in the UK is fairly similar to that in any other developed economy. About 70 per cent of companies employ fewer than 50 people and have a turnover of up to £5 million. Only about 5 or 6 per cent of companies employ more than 250 people or have a turnover of more than £50 million. So most companies that are just starting to export will be small and medium-sized enterprises (SMEs).

Online or traditional exporting?

Nowadays, any company with an e-commerce website can generate some overseas sales. As long as you have a product to ship, you have no limits to your business area. If your company is well promoted and your website attracts attention via search engines, there is no reason why your company cannot pick up some business from anywhere in the world. Using your e-commerce site to generate some export sales is perhaps a first step, and for some companies it may be the perfect way to proceed. But for most companies the internet is only one of many channels to market or to getting their product in front of their potential customers.

How to get started

Whichever way you decide to expand your export business you need to adopt a planned and structured approach. You need to get professional export advice. As we have seen, the governments of all major countries offer a range of services to support their exporters.

We have said that moving into export is a big step for any business and by no means an easy option. So the first thing to do is to honestly assess whether you are ready and able to take on the challenge and move ahead. But where do you actually start and what should you do first?

Starting and progressing with exporting is an iterative process. Even though some things will happen in parallel I would suggest that you try to take one step at a time and work through the following list:

1. Prepare a list of the reasons why you want to start exporting and decide whether it would be the right thing to do.
2. Carry out an 'export audit' of your company, your internal organisation, your products.
3. Assess whether you are ready to start exporting.
4. Develop your export strategy.

Only then should you start to prepare your detailed export plan.

Even at this stage, it is worthwhile contacting your government support organisation and speaking to a local advisor.

Why do you want to start exporting?

If you are having problems with declining sales, a tired product range and limited resources, then exporting is not for you. Exporting is a way of growing a successful business, not a way of getting out of trouble. It is very important to consider why you want to export and what the benefits would be for your company, before you start your export activities. You need to be clear as to why exporting should be a priority for your business and what the real benefits would be. You need to be sure that exporting fits in with your company's short-, medium- and long-term goals. You also need to have a clear definition of what your export product would be.

The reasons why you may decide to start exporting could include any of the following:

- It will increase the size of the potential market for your products and give you a wider and more stable customer base.
- The increase in sales should give you economies of scale in your manufacturing.
- In addition to overall economies of scale, increased sales of some products that have limited sales at present could make these products viable in the long term.
- It could increase the lifetime of some of your products.
- For some products there will never be a large enough market just in one country, and exporting could provide a justification for developing a new product that would not be viable if you had to rely on your domestic market alone.
- Perhaps with your type of product you can take advantage of seasonal demand in other areas of the world. (This is particularly the case with seasonal food products such as high-range fruit and vegetables that can be shipped cost-effectively by air.)

The following reasons would not justify moving into exporting:

- Head office think it would be a good idea.
- We are losing money and need to increase our level of sales.

To help make your decision, you should ask yourself the following questions:

- What does our company expect to gain from exporting? What are our objectives?
- Is exporting consistent with the company's goals?
- How committed is top management to the idea of moving into exporting? Will they be prepared to live with low profitability or even losses in the early stages?

- Do we have the necessary financial and personnel resources to start exporting?
- If we put a major effort into exporting, will our domestic business suffer?
- Are our current products or services suitable for export markets, or would major modifications be required?
- Are the benefits we expect to get from exporting worth the cost and investment involved?
- Would we be better off using our resources to develop new domestic business?

In fact for many companies, the decision will not be made from a zero base. Many companies find that they are starting to get enquiries from overseas, either directly or through their website and some of these enquiries may have already turned into some orders.

Assessing whether you are ready to start exporting

The export readiness checklist

There are a number of key issues that a company's management needs to consider that will help to determine whether a company is ready to commence exporting or whether alternative strategies are better suited to its current position.

Business Victoria, the business support organisation for the State of Victoria, Australia, has produced an excellent Export Readiness Checklist, available to download at their website: **http:// export.business.vic.gov.au/getting-started/export-readiness-checklist**. They list the key issues to be considered as:

- *Commitment.* Is the business prepared to devote the necessary time, effort and resources required for export success? Will the board and CEO give their full backing to exporting as a core business activity?

- *Product/Service.* Will the business be able to identify and exploit market niches based on unique product or service features and qualities? Can the product design be modified if necessary to accommodate market requirements?
- *Marketing.* Does the business have strong marketing skills and a proven track record in its domestic market? Is there high-quality marketing material that could be translated if necessary?
- *Management.* Does the business have sufficient management capabilities to develop and service export markets, or could skills be acquired if necessary?
- *Production.* Does the business have adequate surplus capacity or the flexibility to expand production quickly to service exports? Would the business consider alternative forms of market entry?
- *Finance.* Does the business have sufficient financial strength and resources to develop new overseas markets? Initial items of expenditure may include advertising, promotional material, training and the cost of market visits.

Apart from using your checklist, you can visit a number of government websites that have online questionnaires to assess your 'export readiness'. These include the UKTI interactive tool 'Are you ready to export?' at **www.businesslink.gov.uk**, and the US Department of Commerce online readiness assessment at **www.export.gov/begin/assessment.asp**. These are useful free resources, because their questionnaires can be accessed and completed by anyone – not just UK or US citizens. When you complete the questionnaire you get an immediate assessment. It is no surprise that the conclusion of the assessment is never going to be that your company is not ready to export. It will tell you that you are 'ready to export', 'almost there', 'well on the way', 'have made a good beginning' or are 'on the right track'. But it will also give you a lot of useful information and explain how you can get assistance to address some of the areas of weakness highlighted by the assessment.

The export audit

Just because you can see an opportunity to expand your business by exporting does not mean that you are ready to do so. You may not have the resources to take on the extra work. Even if you have the financial resources, you may well not have the people in place to do the work. In order to decide whether exporting is the right thing for your company to do at this moment in time, you need to carry out an export audit. The results of the audit will give you an idea of what additional resources you will need, and then you can work out what the additional costs will be.

An export audit is carried out like any other type of marketing audit, but from the point of view of developing an export activity.

The areas of your business that you should look at are:

- **export sales history (if any);**
- **potential overseas markets;**
- **applicable products;**
- **sales staffing levels and experience;**
- **finance experience and requirements;**
- **logistics experience and requirements.**

A useful way to proceed is to prepare a simple checklist that you can work through and complete. The exact detail will vary, depending on your business, but a typical example is given below:

1. Sales history

Give details of any overseas sales received over the last three years by value (including margins where available) by:

- **country;**
- **customer;**
- **product.**

2. Potential overseas markets

List any potential overseas markets that you are considering and give reasons why. For instance, have you been contacted by potential customers from these markets? Do you know of competitor activity?

3. Applicable products

Which of your products would you consider selling overseas? Do you think that they are suitable without modification?

4. Sales personnel

- **Do any of your sales personnel (either internal or external) have experience of dealing with overseas sales either with your company or with previous employees?**
- **Do any of your sales personnel speak any foreign language? If so, which language and what is their level of competence?**

5. Finance

For any of the above overseas orders, how have you handled finance/payment?

- **Did you always receive payment in advance?**
- **If not, do your personnel have experience of chasing overseas payments?**
- **Do any personnel have experience of dealing with Letters of Credit?**
- **Do you have any foreign currency accounts?**

6. Logistics

Do any personnel have experience of:

- **export packing;**
- **export shipping;**
- **export paperwork.**

Making the decision

So you understand why you, your company management and key personnel want to start exporting. You have carried out an export audit and now have a clear idea of the additional resources that you will require to start exporting and an estimate of the extra costs to your business. You also have an idea as to whether your product is going to be suitable for export markets. Is it just a yes/no decision? The answer is no. Nowadays there are number of ways that you can start exporting.

Your choices are:

- *Domestic exporting.* Many companies are already selling products that are being exported, although they may not be aware of it. If you are supplying components or ancillary products to a major domestic manufacturer, your products may already be being exported in complete units or plant that that manufacturer is supplying to their overseas customers. If a company becomes aware that this is happening, the next step would be to actively seek out companies that could include its products in equipment that they export, and to also look for domestic buyers who represent or purchase on behalf of foreign companies.
- *Online or e-commerce exporting.* Exporting your products by selling them online is another option that many companies use, particularly as an initial export strategy. This is covered in detail in Chapter 8.
- *Indirect exporting.* This involves entering into a contractual relationship with an intermediary. The intermediary could be: an agent who represents a number of indirect exporters who are not in direct competition with each other; an export management company that will export products on your behalf, gather market information and arrange shipping and documentation; or an export trading company, which will handle all the aspects handled by an export management company but may also provide distribution and storage facilities in the overseas market itself.
- *Direct exporting.* This is what most people understand as exporting. It involves selling your product or service to overseas customers

either directly or through agents or distributors in the overseas market. This is the best way for most companies to export their products, but it also requires the most additional resources.

These different approaches to exporting are explained in much more detail in Chapter 5.

Selecting potential export markets

Depending on which definition you use, there are between 180 and 200 separate countries in the world. When you consider exporting, it is important to consider the cost-effectiveness of building up sales in one market rather than another. If you are only starting in export, you need very good reasons for developing the African or South American markets before you develop your sales in Western Europe or the United States. (Unless of course you are based in an African or South American country, in which case it would be your logical choice.)

Before looking at potential export markets you need to understand why you are successful in your domestic market. A clear understanding of your existing market and the reasons why you are successful there can help you to eliminate some countries that are clearly inappropriate for you. So ask yourself:

- Why do your domestic customers choose your product? Is it because of the quality? The price? Is it because of the reputation of your company and your product? Or is it the quality of your after-sales service?
- What type of product do you supply and what do your customers do with it? Is it an end product in its own right? Is it incorporated into the customers' equipment or product? Is it a service?
- What alternatives exist that your customers could buy instead of your product?
- Are any of your major competitors overseas companies? If so they will almost certainly be very strong in their own domestic market, so you may want to eliminate this from your list of potential target markets.

The world market

According to the International Monetary Fund (IMF), the size of the world economy was about $68 trillion in 2011, and 12 economies account for more than two-thirds of the world's output. The measure of a country's wealth is its gross domestic product (GDP). Figures 2.1 to 2.3 show the International Monetary Fund's estimated figures for GDP at market exchange rates for 2011 for major countries and the EU.

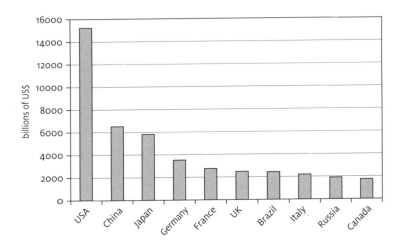

Figure 2.1   GDP data for the top ten world economies

Which country first?

When you evaluate potential export markets, an important factor to consider is their 'similarity' to your existing market. If they exhibit many of the same characteristics as your own market, your product is more likely to be accepted and the channels to market would probably also be similar. You need to consider potential export markets in terms of both their 'size' and the 'ease' of doing business there. Size is not just related to the size of the population. The size of the 'potentially available market' is the most important thing.

Some of the factors that would determine the likely demand for your product in a target country include such things as:

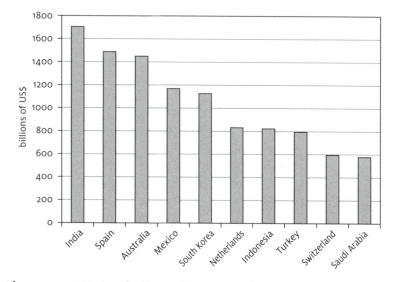

Figure 2.2 GDP data for the next ten economies

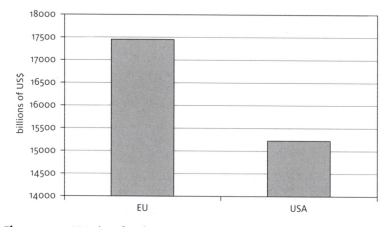

Figure 2.3 GDP data for the European Union and the United States of America

- The size of market for your type of product or similar products (if it is available).
- The population and its structure. The size of the 'economically available' population. Does it have a large middle class with higher levels of disposable income?
- The economic climate. Is it favourable?
- Cultural or climatic issues that may drive the market.
- The level of development, measured by such things as education and literacy, computer literacy and IT readiness.
- The infrastructure – both the transport infrastructure and the IT infrastructure.

Remember that you cannot define the size of the market in purely geographic terms. You need to segment the market and identify the segments of the market that contain your potential customers. The segmentation could be by size of a particular industry or by type of customer.

Factors that can help you to determine how 'easy' it may be for your company to enter the market could include:

- *Language.* This will affect your sales literature and advertising as well as contact with customers in the market.
- *Political stability.* Is the country stable? Are there any risks?
- *Legal and regulatory issues.* Are there any legal or regulatory barriers to entry? Does your product comply with local standards?
- *Import duties/tariffs.* Is there a preferential tariff arrangement between your country and the target market? Are there any barriers to trade?
- *Distance to the market.* This will certainly be a factor if your products are low-value/high-volume.
- *Competition.* Is there strong local competition for your type of product? If a company from your target country is a serious rival in your domestic market, you need to consider whether you will be able to compete with them on their own ground.

It is frequently not possible to decide whether a particular export market is right for your company and your products until you have carried out a certain amount of research into the market. For this reason it is usual for a company to select a number of 'potential target' markets and to research these markets in parallel.

You need to establish selection criteria and score each potential target market against them. Once sufficient research has been carried out, you will be able to 'score' each market against your criteria on the basis of the likely demand for your product and the relative ease of entering the market for your company. The markets that score the highest against your selection criteria will be the ones that you select for more detailed market research.

Rating charts

If you have no experience of selecting markets, I strongly recommend that you have a discussion with your local trade adviser, who will help you to decide on the criteria that are most important to your business and your type of product, and will also guide you towards selecting sensible initial target markets.

If you are putting a selection chart together yourself, I would suggest that you keep the list of criteria to fewer than 20 and that you split the chart into two sections. An inexperienced exporter does not want to have to deal with difficult markets, and the criteria in Section 1 would allow you to decide whether it is worth moving down to Section 2 of the chart for that particular target market. The criteria in this section would require a simple yes or no answer and would include such things as political stability, import restrictions or barriers, and legal issues or regulations. The two sections are shown in Tables 2.1 and 2.2.

A negative answer to any of the criteria in Section 1 would almost certainly eliminate the country from the list of potential target markets. Section 2 of the selection chart (Table 2.2) would be used to compare the countries that have not been eliminated in Section 1. Each of the questions would be answered by using a score of between 1 and 5 (5 being the most positive).

Most new exporters start with markets that are relatively easy to deal with. In fact many companies begin exporting by selling their products to customers in neighbouring countries or countries with a common language, and many countries have built up strong trade links with their

Table 2.1 Country selection chart: Section 1

Criteria	Yes	No
Political: is the country stable?		
Economic: is the economic climate favourable?		
Is it likely to remain so?		
Non-tariff barriers: are there any major trade barriers – quotas, import restrictions?		
Tariffs: are import tariffs or taxes so high as to make our local pricing uncompetitive?		
Local standards: do we need to get any local testing certification for our product?		
Product protection: do we need to get patent/ trademark protection before proceeding?		
Safety: is the country safe to visit?		

Table 2.2 Country selection chart: Section 2

Country	A	B	C	D	E
Size of market:					
Market demand/growth potential:					
Population/structure:					
Level of development:					
Transportation to market:					
Transport infrastructure:					
Product acceptability:					
Level of competition:					
Language:					
Local business practices:					
Cultural issues:					

neighbours or with other countries within their own trading region or trading block. There is a high level of trade between countries within the European Union (EU), between the United States and Canada, between Australia and New Zealand. Within the EU, there is a very high level of trade between the UK and the Republic of Ireland, and the same is true of trade between Austria and Germany and among the Scandinavian countries. Although there may be some differences, the things that make these markets easier to deal with are common languages, common standards and historical traditions. New exporters tend to try the easiest markets first, before moving on to more challenging or distant markets. Developing countries are riskier to deal with and are probably best left until you have more experience.

If you are an Australian company, you may begin with New Zealand or target one of the more developed economies in Asia. Companies in African countries are also likely to choose another African country as their first export market.

How many countries should you initially target?

Different markets have different requirements. Your products may require additional certification or modifications to be suitable for some markets, yet be perfectly suitable for other markets as they are. Trying to export to a number of widely different markets can be expensive in both time and money. Most companies that are starting in exporting focus on one or two individual target countries. In a large country like Germany or the United States you may even decide to concentrate initially on one region. The advice is clear. Start exporting to one or two target countries and develop your sales in these. Make sure that you have the resources in place to continue to service and develop these markets before you move on to others.

Industry sectors and clusters

You may also choose to target a particular export market because that country has an industry sector that uses your type of product. A country such as Norway, although only number 24 in the world in terms of the size of its economy, could be a very good choice for you if you manufacture and sell equipment to the offshore oil and gas industry.

In fact many governments target much of their export support by industry sectors as much as by country or region. UKTI in the UK takes this approach (most UK trade missions are sector-specific) as does the Australia Trade Commission (Austrade) in Australia and the Department of Trade and Industry (DTI) in South Africa.

Product considerations

Although exporting can be a catalyst for innovation and developing new or modified products, clearly it would be ideal if you could sell your existing products, with minimum modification, into your initial target markets. In deciding which country to target as your first export market, your product is crucial. Some goods may sell anywhere, but you will be surprised at the range not just of local rules and regulations, but also of local or cultural preferences that decide whether your existing product will sell, or even whether it may be legally offered for sale in some overseas markets.

Local regulations can affect everything from the labelling and the certification of foodstuffs and medical products to regulations for machinery and electrical goods.

3

Researching overseas markets

Every overseas market is different. It is essential to research your target markets before you start to promote and sell your products or services within them. To give yourself the best possible chance of successfully entering a market, you need to understand both the market itself and how your product will fit into it.

To do this, you need to carry out both market research and marketing research. Market research is research about markets. Marketing research involves not just collecting information about your markets but also analysing it in the context of the marketing of your products.

Market research data consists of primary and secondary data. Primary data is obtained from primary sources: that is, directly in the marketplace. You can obtain it either by carrying out field research directly yourself or by commissioning a consultant or market research company to carry out the fieldwork for you. Secondary data is not obtained directly from fieldwork, and market research based on secondary data sources is referred to as 'desk research'.

How to plan your marketing research

Before you start to collect any information, you need to decide on your objectives and put together a plan for your market research. It is important to plan how you will do it so as to make sure that you obtain all of the information that you need. Much time, effort and cost can be wasted by starting an export market research project without defining the objectives.

The key steps to carrying out the marketing research are as follows:

1. Define the objectives.
2. Decide what information needs to be obtained.
3. Decide the best way of obtaining it.
4. Collect the data.
5. Analyse the data.

The objectives

The objectives must be clearly defined. This should explain why the research is being conducted and should also include the timescale that is necessary for completion of the work. The objective could be:

> *To obtain information that will enable us to decide whether or not to enter a new overseas market.*

But it could also have a more specific objective related to one or more aspects of market entry.

The information required

A list should be prepared, detailing all of the information required. This needs to be a complete list of everything needed, because it is extremely costly to have to go back later to collect additional information that was not considered in the first place.

How to obtain the information

You can obtain a lot of basic information about your target market by carrying out desk research. But in most cases this will need to be supplemented by some fieldwork in the market itself. You need to use someone who fully understands the business and will be able to understand the methods of marketing research, as well as the full objectives of the project.

Collecting the data

Collecting the data involves using the methods and the data sources detailed later in this chapter. Some key sources of information are listed under 'Useful websites' on page 138.

Analysing the data

Where specific projects such as customer surveys, market analysis or competitor analysis have been carried out, the data that have been collected need to be verified and analysed. The assumptions used in interpreting the data need to be stated. Data analysis must be carried out by your marketing professional (this may be you personally). It is important to remember that the analysis of the data will only be as good as the understanding of the person carrying it out.

Once all of the material has been analysed, the key information needs to be put into a research report that can be used as a reference document for preparing your export plan.

Carrying out marketing research for overseas markets

The principles of carrying out marketing research for export markets are the same as those applicable in your domestic market, but the market and the marketing environment will almost certainly be different. In your domestic market you might carry out field research yourself or you might commission a consultant or market research company to do it for you. The same is true for overseas markets, but it is advantageous if any report is supplemented by your visiting the market personally.

You need to learn about the customers who will buy your product and how they currently buy equivalent products. You need to understand who the competitors are and how they operate within the market. You need to look at and consider:

- the country type and population structure;
- the infrastructure;
- legal and regulatory issues;
- the market size;
- the industry structure within the market;
- the major customers for your type of product and their needs, usage and attitudes;
- the suitability of your product – whether it is suitable for the market as it is or if any modifications will be required to make it saleable;
- the way you will market the product;
- distribution channels;
- competition.

Country type

When researching target countries you need to consider a number of factors:

- The size of your potential market could be limited by the size of the population or by the size of the 'economically available' population in your target country.
- Political situation – is the country stable? What type of government does it have and could political changes adversely affect the local business climate?
- Economic climate – is this favourable and likely to remain so?
- Safety – how safe is it to visit, stay in or live in the target country? Are there high levels of crime? Is there a risk of terrorist activity?
- Legal issues – are there any local standards or regulations that would affect your existing or future products?

The infrastructure

- Communications – does your target market have widespread access to telephones or the internet?
- Internal travel – how good is the internal transport system within the country?
- Transportation – are there good transport links to the target market by ship? By air? By other means?

Legal and regulatory issues

- Are there any barriers to accessing the market? Consider import duties, taxes, quotas, language, other government legislation and so on.
- Does your product comply with local standards? Is any local testing or certification required?
- What is the patent situation? Do you have local trademark protection? Are there any other risks to your intellectual property?
- Is new legislation or new regulation likely?

The market size

- How big is it in value or volume terms?
- Will it be affected by future trends? These might include the population moving from the land to cities, a growing middle class or an aging population.
- The state of the market – is it a new market? A mature market? A saturated market?
- Are new areas of the market developing?

The industry structure within the market

- How is the market segmented/structured?
- How is the target industry geographically distributed? What are the key areas/regions?
- Are there a few large players, many small ones or a mixture?
- Are the target companies private or public sector?
- Is the market more or less advanced than your domestic market?

The major customers for your type of product and their needs, usage and attitudes

- Who are the main customers?
- Where are they located?
- Who are the main suppliers and what do customers think of them?
- Why will they buy from you? Do they see a need for your product/service?
- What influences their purchasing decisions?
- How much are customers prepared to pay for your type of product?

The suitability of your product

- Is your product/service acceptable to this market in its current form or are modifications required?
- What are the main competing products? Are they directly comparable?
- Could cultural influences affect the way that your product will be perceived in this market place? A basic product in some markets may be a luxury item in another. A different perception of your product will mean that your marketing approach will need to be different.

The way you will market the product

- What methods of sales promotion are used in the market place?
- What methods of communication are used? Press, TV, internet, e-mail, direct mail?

Distribution channels

- How is the market supplied?
- What channels of distribution are available?
- Are agents or distributors used within the market?
- Is there local legislation relating to agents or distributors?
- What are the costs of distribution?

Competition

- Who are the key competitors?
- Are they local suppliers or international competitors?
- What products do they manufacture/sell?
- Are they more or less sophisticated than your company?
- What are their strengths and weaknesses?
- What are their marketing and pricing strategies?

Carrying out the research yourself

The first thing that you need to do is to prepare a checklist. A checklist is important for two reasons. Firstly, it can be extremely costly to have to go back later to collect additional information because it was not considered in the first place. Secondly, the problem for exporters is not that there is too little information available. It is that there is so much that it is difficult to pinpoint the data that are really relevant. A checklist helps you to avoid collecting large amounts of irrelevant information. Ask yourself why you need specific information and what you will do with it. If you do not know, then you do not need it.

Your checklist should detail all of the information that you need to obtain and the headings would form the main headings in the final report. A typical checklist for a target market could include the following main headings:

- market size;
- market structure and segmentation;
- market trends;
- market share;
- selling and distribution methods;
- marketing communication methods;
- product requirements;
- company/industry image;
- user attitudes and behaviour;
- local pricing;
- competition.

Under each of these headings would be a list of the information required or the questions that your research needs to answer.

Desk research

Desk research involves the collection of data that are already available from existing sources. Huge amounts of information are available on most markets. Much of this information is free or relatively inexpensive. Trips to other countries can be expensive, so it is important that you obtain as much from published information as you can, before you actually visit your target market.

It is clearly a waste of money to carry out or commission research to obtain information that is already available in the form of a ready-made report. Many reports, particularly those produced by government departments or non-profit-making organisations, are available free of charge and many government support organisations provide a wealth of basic information on individual export markets. Much of this information can be printed off or downloaded as PDF files from individual websites for free. Although for some services you have to register on the site, much of the information can be accessed by anyone from any country. A list of websites is included in the 'Useful websites' section at the end of this book.

The value of desk research when deciding on export markets is that you can often find enough information to make an initial decision as to whether a particular target market looks promising or is just not suitable for your company or your product. If your product is sold into a particular industry sector, you can often find enough information by desk research to decide whether that industry sector is large enough in one target market to justify entry into that market rather than another.

Types of data and reports

There are a number of types of published data that can be used to provide you with information relating to markets and industry sectors as well as statistical information on exports and imports of specific types of products for different markets. The main types are country (market) reports, industry (sector) reports, company information, and product or statistical information.

Sources of information

Much information can be obtained via the internet. Key sources of information include:

- market reports and sector reports for export markets (available from UK Trade & Investment, www.ukti.gov.uk, the US Commercial Service, www.export.gov, or Austrade, www.austrade.gov.au);
- ready-made reports (from specialist market research companies such as Key Note, www.keynote.co.uk; Euromonitor, www.euromonitor.com; Mintel, www.mintel.co.uk; and Frost & Sullivan, www.frost.com);
- government statistics and Prodcom reports (eg UK statistics from the Office for National Statistics, www.ons.gov.uk);
- European statistics (Eurostat, http://epp.eurostat.ec.europa.eu);
- other statistical information (eg Food and Agriculture Organisation (FAO), www.fao.org);
- company and industry information (companies such as Kompass, www.kompass.co.uk, or Kelly's, www.kellysearch.com or from Companies House, www.companieshouse.gov.uk);
- trade associations (find details of trade associations for your industry from the Trade Association Forum, www.taforum.org);
- your local Chambers of Commerce (www.britishchambers.org.uk for the UK) and also the World Chambers Network, www.worldchambers.com, which is the official portal of Chambers of Commerce with details of over 14,000 Chambers of Commerce worldwide;
- industry-specific websites such as www.lfra.co.uk (for the food industry) and www.poyry.com (pulp & paper). Also Net Resources International (NRI), www.nridigital.com, which has separate sections for 25 different industries covering 85 countries.

Field research

Once you have obtained all of the material you can get from desk research, you can decide whether you also need to carry out field research in your target market. Field research involves visiting the target market and can also mean carrying out face-to-face interviews with potential customers, agents or distributors. You can of course visit your target market on your own, but if you have limited experience of doing business overseas you would gain more from visiting as part of an organised group, as part of a trade mission or for an exhibition.

Sector-focused trade missions

Sector-focused trade missions typically last between three and eight days and are usually organised by a government agency such as a Chamber of Commerce. The missions are often specific to a particular industry or event. They are an ideal way to visit a market that you are unfamiliar with and you can gain from the experience of the mission leader and others on the mission as well as from the local contacts that you make.

Tradeshows and exhibitions

Visiting or taking part in a tradeshow or overseas exhibition specific to your industry is an ideal way of finding out a lot about that industry in your target country. Although you can get an idea of the products being sold in the market and the competition just by visiting the exhibition, if you actually take part in one you have much more opportunity to meet and talk with potential customers.

Using an agency to carry out market research

Using a professional market research agency to carry out market research will obviously be more expensive than doing the work yourself. But if you and your staff are inexperienced in doing market research it may well prove to be more cost-effective. They will probably complete the task more quickly and will have the skills to make sure that all parts of the task are completed properly. They can research the market anonymously and they may already have secondary data (or access to secondary data) available from previous work that they have carried out in the target market. If they are locally based or use local personnel in the target market, they will bring local knowledge to the task, and since they do not work for your company, respondents in interviews may be more open in their replies.

Additionally, your own company personnel do not need to spend so much time on the project, so they can get on with their normal jobs.

As with any work that you commission, unless you are already familiar with the agency and have used them before, you should get quotations from a number of different organisations before deciding which one to go with. (In some markets, however, this may not be possible as there may only be one agency with a good reputation and experience in the field that interests you.)

The marketing research brief

If you are commissioning market research you need to prepare a research brief to inform the potential agencies of the aims and objectives of your research project. The brief should explain why you want the research to be carried out and detail the information that you need to obtain from it. It is important that everything is clearly stated in the brief to ensure that the final report will provide the information and recommendations that will help you to take your decisions.

The brief should include the following:

- **introduction;**
- **scope;**
- **purpose;**
- **information required;**
- **timescales;**
- **progress reporting;**
- **reporting requirements;**
- **notes.**

The research brief should be discussed with the agencies, which may make suggestions based on their own experience. They may see areas of research or information that you have omitted to ask for that will be needed if you are to take certain decisions, and may suggest extending or reducing the scope of the project or changing its emphasis in some way.

Choosing the agency to work with

The agencies will put together their proposals for your evaluation. You need to be sure that you understand exactly what they are offering and that their proposal shows that they have clearly understood your brief. Generally, you want to be sure that the project will be carried out in accordance with the Market Research Society's Code of Conduct. You can find this on the Market Research Society's website, **www.marketresearch.org.uk**.

The proposal

There are a number of key points that you would expect to see or confirm in the proposal. The most important is that the agency demonstrates that it clearly understands your brief and exactly what you expect to get out of their research. You should make sure that the following are also included in their proposal:

- **a detailed list of the information that their research will provide;**
- **the proposed methodology;**
- **the scope of the study;**
- **the qualifications and experience of the researchers;**
- **the timescale of the project;**
- **the total cost of the project;**
- **whether there will be any progress reports or interim meetings;**
- **specific areas where they expect to be able to make recommendations;**
- **the number of copies of the final report included in the price;**
- **written assurances of both exclusivity and confidentiality.**

The report

The overall report that you receive should bring all of the information together in a clear and concise form. A suggested format for a research report is shown below:

- **background;**
- **scope;**
- **project objectives;**

- methodology;
- main findings;
- summary of findings and conclusions;
- recommendations;
- appendix.

Using companies based in the target market

Depending on the type of market that you are looking at, you may decide to commission research from a company based in the target market itself. A local company clearly has advantages because it is actually in the market and you would expect its personnel to know how the market functions. But it can be more difficult to get a good proposal put together and it may not be easy to judge the quality of the personnel who will carry out the work, because you will not want to go to the expense of visiting them and they in turn will not want the cost of visiting you before they have a contract. My suggestion is that you should consider local companies, but make sure that you can get a sensible recommendation, either from other companies that have used them before or through your local embassy in the target market.

Government support for market research

Apart from compiling market and sector reports, some governments also offer their exporters assistance for export market research projects. Small businesses in particular may be eligible for financial support. UK Trade & Investment, the US Department of Commerce and Austrade all have such schemes, which can be an excellent way for companies to obtain free independent advice on how to get the most out of a marketing research project. They can advise on points such as:

- **how to conduct marketing research;**
- **locating and briefing market research agencies;**
- **evaluating their proposals and reports;**
- **identifying published reports and undertaking desk research;**
- **planning a field trip, setting up appointments and conducting interviews;**
- **analysing data, drawing conclusions and writing a report.**

4

Export strategies and export plans

Any company that decides to start exporting needs to develop an export strategy. This should be easily understood by all company personnel and should provide a clear idea of why you are exporting and what you expect to achieve. From your export strategy you can develop your export plan. This is a marketing plan for export markets and will define how entry into these markets will be made. It needs to include your specific marketing objectives and the marketing strategies and tactics necessary to achieve them. It should also include details of the resources that will be required – both personnel and financial resources as well as an adequate budget to cover the export start-up costs.

Developing your export strategy

Successful exporters always know exactly why they are exporting and the results and benefits that they expect to achieve. Having an export strategy that everyone in the company understands and supports is just as important to a small company as it is to a large one. A sound export strategy:

- shows that your company is developing its business in a professional way;
- provides direction to your staff;
- ensures that those who were involved in developing the strategy will buy into it and support it;
- is a useful tool when dealing with your bank and with government support agencies.

The starting point in developing your export strategy is to identify the key factors that influenced your decision to start exporting. You need to make a list of all the issues that made you decide to export, discuss them with key members of staff and rank them in order of importance to the success of your business. Choose the five most important factors from this list and develop your export strategy around them. Develop the full strategy and write it down. The written document should be clear and concise and should be relatively short.

The marketing planning process

The principles of marketing planning are used in the process of developing an export plan. Depending on where you are in terms of developing your overseas business, the process can be used to:

- prepare the justification for starting to export;
- prepare a basic export plan;
- put together a complete company export plan to be included in the business plan;
- prepare an export plan for an individual target market;
- prepare an argument for introducing a new product in certain overseas markets;
- revamp the marketing approach for existing products for overseas markets.

The way that you use the marketing planning process to prepare an export plan will be different from preparing a normal marketing plan for your domestic market. It is easier to split the process into a number of individual phases and to work on these consecutively. These are research and analysis, preparing objectives and strategies, calculating costs and budgets, preparing and presenting the written plan, and implementing it.

Research and situation analysis

- Evaluate and select the target markets.
- Carry out marketing research within the company and in the target markets.
- Look at the company's strengths and weaknesses with regard to exporting to the target markets.
- Look at the product's/service's strengths and weaknesses with regard to exporting.
- Select and price the products/services for the target markets.

Objectives and strategies

- Make relevant assumptions.
- Set specific marketing objectives for each target market.
- Define changes to internal organisation and procedures.
- Generate marketing strategies and tactics.
- Decide market entry strategies and distribution methods.
- Forecast sales to be achieved in the target markets together with the timescale for achieving them.
- Define programmes to be carried out.

Costs and budgets

- Cost up resource requirements and programmes.
- Set budgets and prepare a partial profit-and-loss account.
- Review the results and revise the objectives, strategies or programmes.

The written plan

- Write the plan.
- Present the plan.

Implementation schedule

- **Prepare master schedule.**
- **Review and update procedures.**

Marketing planning is an iterative process and the export plan should be reviewed and updated as it is implemented. More detailed information on marketing planning can be found in my book *How to Write a Marketing Plan*, published by Kogan Page.

Situation analysis

In previous chapters, we have explained how to evaluate and select target markets and how to research them. However, marketing research involves not just collecting information about your markets, but also analysing it in the context of the marketing of your products. Situation analysis is the process that helps you to analyse information and present it in a way that you can use for planning. It can be used to:

- **review the economic and business climate in your target markets;**
- **look at the strengths and weaknesses of your company – its organisation, its performance and its key products;**
- **compare the company with its competitors;**
- **identify opportunities and threats.**

You should carry out both an internal and an external review, and also review your product or service. In your internal review you should examine your company structure, processes and objectives, and identify both strengths and weaknesses as they relate to your readiness and ability to export. Assess your management, marketing, logistics and financial functions in the same way. The external review will look first at any domestic external factors that may impact on your ability to export. You should then look at your target markets to see which offer the best prospects for your company and its products. You should also carry out a review of the key competitors that will be present in your target markets. Finally, you should look at your existing products or services and assess whether they can be marketed in the target markets as they are or whether they would require modification or additional certification. The key process used in situation analysis is SWOT analysis. It is a simple tool that can be used to analyse the information that you have gathered in your internal, external and product reviews. SWOT stands for:

Strengths and Weaknesses as they relate to our Opportunities and Threats in the marketplace.

The strengths and weaknesses refer to your company and its products and should be identified from the internal and product reviews. The opportunities and threats are usually taken to be external factors over which your company has no control and the external review will reveal them. The strengths and opportunities support the objective, while the weaknesses and threats are detrimental to it.

In carrying out SWOT analysis it is usual to list the strengths, weaknesses, opportunities and threats on the same page. This is done by segmenting the page into four squares, and entering strengths and weaknesses in the top squares and opportunities and threats in the bottom ones as shown in Table 4.1.

Table 4.1 Presentation of SWOT analysis

STRENGTHS	WEAKNESSES
....	....
....	....
....	....
....	....
....	....
OPPORTUNITIES	**THREATS**
....	....
....	....
....	....
....	....
....	....

Pricing for export markets

You cannot assume that the pricing levels that you have for your product/service in your domestic market will be right for overseas markets. You may sell direct to your customers in your domestic market, but will probably have to consider selling through an importer or distributor if you are exporting. There will also be additional costs to ship your product to your overseas markets and for some markets there will also be import duties to pay. Setting export prices for products and services is a key issue for all exporters and may decide whether exporting is viable or not.

The most common methods of setting export prices are:

- *Cost-plus pricing.* The export selling price is determined by adding the extra costs of exporting to the domestic manufacturing cost. The extra costs would include such things as export packaging, freight and documentation costs, customs duties and distribution costs. While cost-plus pricing is simple to use, the resulting prices could easily make your product or service uncompetitive.
- *Top-down pricing.* With top-down pricing the prices are calculated by working back from the market price that you believe you will have to meet in order to be competitive. Using the top-down method to calculate the optimum ex-works price can sometimes result in a calculated price level that would be difficult to sell to top management. In such cases, companies need to be realistic, and this is where marginal costing comes in.
- *Marginal costing/pricing.* The technique of marginal costing treats export sales as additional business that makes a reduced contribution to a company's fixed costs. The same product is sold at a lower ex-works price when it is exported than when it is being sold in the domestic market. Marginal costing is based on separating your costs into fixed and variable costs and only allocating those costs that vary directly with the level of activity to the product or service. Fixed costs are not allocated to units of sales or production, but are treated collectively as costs for the period of time being considered. Fixed costs include items such as rent, rates, interest charges, depreciation and administration

costs. Variable costs include only the raw materials, labour and energy costs involved in the production process. (To avoid the risk of being accused of 'dumping' the product, it is important that this does not result in the end selling price of the product in your overseas markets being below the end selling price in your domestic market.)

Objectives and strategies

Assumptions

These are key facts and assumptions that you make when putting the plan together. They should be few in number and should relate only to the key issues that would significantly affect the likelihood of the plan's objectives being achieved. For example:

- The $/£ exchange rate will remain in the range $1.50 to $1.70:£1 for the next 12 months.
- Interest rates will not increase by more than 1 per cent over the next three years.
- Company wage increases will not exceed inflation over the next three years.

Setting your marketing objectives

Objectives are what you want to achieve; strategies are how you get there.

Expanding your sales into overseas markets will involve you selling your existing products into new export markets, but could also include modifying some of your existing products to make them suitable for those markets. Marketing objectives must be definable and quantifiable so that there is an achievable target to aim towards. 'Achievable' is the key word. An objective that is clearly impossible to achieve will be seen as a disincentive by your sales team. Marketing objectives should be defined in such a way that actual performance can be compared with the objective. They should be expressed in terms of values or market shares, and vague terms such as increase, improve or maximise should not be used.

Objectives should always be **SMART**:

- *Specific* – they should be expressed in terms of values or market shares, and vague terms such as increase, improve or maximise should not be used.
- *Measurable* – you should be able to confirm whether you have achieved them or not.
- *Achievable* – are you putting in the resources, in terms of people and investment, to achieve them?
- *Realistic* – although targets should stretch you, if they are clearly unreasonable they will just be demotivating.
- *Time-bound* – there should be a set timescale for achieving every objective.

The following are examples of marketing objectives:

- to increase sales of the product in the United States by 10 per cent per annum in real terms, each year for the next three years;
- to increase market share for the product in Germany from 5 per cent to 10 per cent over three years;
- to increase our export sales of the product by 30 per cent in real terms within five years.

You need to have short-term as well as long-term objectives. Increasing sales by 30 per cent over five years may seem a huge rise, but if you redefine it as increasing sales by 5 or 6 per cent a year, it will appear to be much more achievable.

Your marketing objectives will also translate into sales forecasts for your target markets.

Devising marketing strategies

Strategies are the broad methods chosen to achieve specific objectives. They describe the means of achieving the objectives in the timescale required, but they do not include the detail of the individual courses of action that will be followed on a day-by-day or month-by-month basis. These are *tactics*. So a strategy is the broad definition of how the objective is to be achieved, the action steps are tactics, and the action plans contain the detail of the individual actions, their timing and who will carry them out.

In devising strategies for your export plan it is helpful to think in terms of the 'four Ps':

- *Product* – the benefits that your product offers your potential customers in your target market. Whether it needs to be modified or changed to better meet the requirements of the customers.
- *Pricing* – will you aim to match the local competition? Will you try to beat them on price? Or will you sell at a higher price on the basis of additional benefits that your product offers?
- *Place* – how will you sell your product? Online? Direct to large end users? Through distributors or agents?
- *Promotion* – will you use advertising? Exhibitions? If the local language in your target country is different from yours, you will need to have your sales literature translated.

In looking at strategies it can be useful to expand the 'four Ps' and add:

- *People* – do you need additional staff resources, and will new and existing employees need specialist training?
- *Processes* – do you need to modify your processes and systems to make them more suitable for the requirements of exporting?

Strategies can come from many different sources and it is wise to consider all possible ways of generating them. All of the strategies should be consistent with each other and with the objectives that they are expected to achieve. You should also determine which strategies can be best implemented with the resources and capabilities that your company has or will have over the timescale of the plan.

Tactics and action plans

Your strategies give a broad definition of how an objective is to be achieved, but the action steps are tactics and the action plans contain the detail of the individual actions, their timing and who will carry them out.

If your strategy for pricing was:

Change price, terms or conditions for particular product groups for particular markets,

the tactics could be:

- **Reduce price of product to maximise sales.**
- **Calculate price levels to meet specific pricing policies of competitors.**
- **Set price at 10 per cent below market leader.**
- **Price product high where we have technical advantage over competitors' products.**

Your strategies and tactics need to be turned into programmes or action plans that will enable you to give clear instructions to your staff. Each action plan should include:

- **aims – what to do/where you want to go;**
- **action – what you need to do to get there;**
- **person responsible – who will do it;**
- **start date;**
- **finish date;**
- **budgeted cost.**

Each action plan would need to be broken down into its component parts.

Costs and budgets

To implement your export plan you will incur additional costs. These will include additional salary costs for sales personnel, travel costs for business-related travel, and marketing costs for sales promotional materials and activities. Most companies starting to export set a sensible target for the amount of additional sales that they intend to initially achieve. So if you are expecting to increase your turnover by 10 to 15 per cent over a three-year period, you are unlikely initially to need to take on additional staff for functions such as logistics and finance. As your overall level of sales grows, including the contribution coming from export, you will need to look at making further investments as part of your overall business planning and budgeting processes. But for the purpose of an initial export plan, most companies will only need to prepare an additional profit-and-loss account to cover the additional sales included in the plan.

The written plan

The written plan should only contain the key information that needs to be communicated. It should be clear and concise, and excessive or irrelevant detail should be excluded. The written plan should include summary information resulting from the marketing research that you have carried out relating to your company and your target markets, but the bulk of the detail should be excluded from it, to avoid confusing the reader. A summary of the key action plans should be included, but not smaller sub-plans. Keep the document short. A four- or five-page document will suffice for most plans, although a full plan including profit-and-loss accounts and justifications for capital investment as well as additional revenue expenditure could be longer.

Formats for export marketing plans

There are many different formats that can be adopted for export plans. There are two main types of situation where you need to prepare an export plan, and these two types lend themselves to different formats for the written plan. I differentiate these two types of plan by referring to them as 'the complete export plan' and 'the export marketing plan'.

- *The complete export plan.* **If you are a company that is completely new to exporting or not very experienced, you need to prepare a document that shows why you have decided that you want to export, what your export strategy is, the resources that you have and the new resources that you will add to achieve your new export sales goals. You need to confirm why you have selected your target markets, what changes (if any) need to be made to your product and what you expect to achieve.**
- *The export marketing plan.* **As you become more experienced as an exporter, your export planning will become an integral part of**

your annual planning and budgeting process, so the plans that you prepare will take on the more traditional format of a marketing plan. Your marketing plan for your domestic market and your marketing plan for export markets will become two parallel parts of your annual business plan and your annual budget.

The complete export plan

For this type of plan I favour using the format developed many years ago by the US Department of Commerce. This format is now in use throughout the world and is also promoted by various support organisations in Australia and Canada. Details can be obtained by going to the US government website 'Export.gov', **www.export.gov**. Click on 'Export Basics' and 'Develop your Export Plan' and you will find 'Outline for an Export Plan'.

The outline of this plan format is shown below:

Table of Contents
Executive Summary (one or two pages maximum)
Introduction: Why This Company Should Export
Part 1 – Export Policy Commitment Statement
Part 2 – Situation/Background Analysis

- **Product or Service**
- **Operations**
- **Personnel and Export Organisation**
- **Resources of the Firm**
- **Industry Structure, Competition and Demand**

Part 3 – Marketing Component

- **Identifying, Evaluating and Selecting Target Markets**
- **Product Selection and Pricing**

- **Distribution Methods**
- **Terms and Conditions**
- **Internal Organisation and Procedures**
- **Sales Goals: Profit-and-loss Forecasts**

Part 4 – Tactics: Action Steps

- **Primary Target Countries**
- **Secondary Target Countries**
- **Indirect Marketing Efforts**

Part 5 – Export Budget

- **Pro Forma Financial Statements**

Part 6 – Implementation Schedule

- **Follow-up**
- **Periodic and Management Review (Measuring Results against Plan)**

Addenda: Background Data on Target Countries and Market

- **Basic Market Statistics: Historical and Projected**
- **Background Facts**
- **Competitive Environment**

(**SOURCE:** US Department of Commerce)

This format may look rather complicated, but it follows a logical progression of ideas. Not every company will need to complete information for every one of the individual subheadings, and under other subheadings a sentence or two will suffice.

The export marketing plan

This is the format that I have developed for marketing plans and more details can be found in my book *How to Write a Marketing Plan*, published by Kogan Page. The outline of this plan format is shown below:

1. Introduction.
2. Executive summary.
3. Situation analysis:
   - assumptions;
   - sales (history/budget);
   - key products;
   - strategic markets/industries;
   - key sales areas.
4. Marketing objectives.
5. Marketing strategies.
6. Schedules.
7. Sales promotion.
8. Budgets.
9. Profit-and-loss account.
10. Controls.
11. Update procedures.
12. Appendices.

Depending on the scope of your plan you may need to omit or combine certain sections.

5

Market entry strategies

Having made the decision to enter an overseas market, you need to consider the ways you can go about it and decide which entry strategy is right for your business. The most suitable entry strategy for you will depend on your product and will be influenced by a number of factors, including the size of your business and your willingness to accept risk. The strategy that you adopt may be different for different markets and, depending on your product and the target market, you may need to adopt a combination of entry strategies.

Types of exporting

There are a number of different types of export entry strategies that companies can employ (Figure 5.1).

Passive or 'domestic' exporting

Most companies making a conscious decision to move into exporting are thinking about direct exporting, whether this is from their home base or by means of an intermediary based in the target country itself.

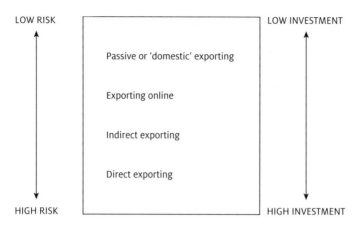

LOW RISK   LOW INVESTMENT

Passive or 'domestic' exporting

Exporting online

Indirect exporting

Direct exporting

HIGH RISK   HIGH INVESTMENT

Figure 5.1 Types of export entry strategy

In fact, although they may not be aware of it, many companies are already selling products that are being exported in complete units or plant that a domestic manufacturer is supplying to its overseas customers. This is called 'passive exporting'. If a company becomes aware that it is passively exporting, the next step would be to actively seek out companies that could include their products in equipment that they export, and to look for domestic buyers who represent or purchase on behalf of foreign companies. This 'domestic' exporting is low risk because the company is selling its product to a domestic buyer or customer who then ships the product abroad and handles all of the documentation and transportation. Apart from original equipment manufacturers (OEMs), examples of this type of domestic customer include civil and mechanical engineering contractors and major multinational companies.

Exporting online

Any company with an e-commerce website can generate some overseas sales. The requirements for order handling and after-sales service for export business are similar when you are dealing with them on- and offline, but there are additional national and international regulations relating to e-commerce. If you want to start exporting by selling your goods online, you need to know what you are doing. You cannot handle overseas business on your website in exactly the same way that you handle domestic sales. We will look at the issues relating to selling online in more detail in Chapter 8.

Indirect approaches to exporting

Indirect exporting provides companies with a way of entering overseas markets without all of the costs and the risks of direct exporting. It involves working completely through an intermediary and not actually handling your export business yourself. The type of intermediary is determined by the level of resource that the company is prepared to commit to their export activity. Some types of intermediary will not only obtain orders on your behalf, but will also handle all of the export documentation and even shipping arrangements. Others will only obtain the orders, so that you still have to have your own staff who can handle the documentation and logistics. But by engaging in indirect exporting, a company does not have to invest in sales personnel experienced in travelling and selling abroad or in the cost of export travel. The main forms of indirect exporting are through export agents, export management companies or export trading companies.

Export agents usually operate by representing a number of indirect exporters who are not in direct competition with each other. Some types of export agent purchase products direct from the manufacturer, repackage them and sell them overseas in their own name. Others sell the products through their own contacts overseas and are paid a commission on the sales that they generate.

Export management companies act as either agents or distributors and provide additional services on a commission or a retainer basis. Some export management companies offer their client companies the facilities of a complete export department and some of the larger export management companies will even take title to the goods and export on their own account. The services offered include organising shipping and handling export documentation.

Export trading companies may also offer access to distribution channels and storage facilities. Much trade with South Korea and Japan is conducted through export trading houses such as Hyundai, Samsung, Mitsubishi and Mitsui.

It is quite common for a company to adopt a strategy by which they develop direct export business with markets that are easier to manage and use indirect methods for selling to other more difficult markets. So a European company may start by selling directly and through distribution to customers within the European Union and to countries such as the United States and Australia, but use an export agent or export management company for sales to Africa and the Middle East.

Direct approaches to exporting

Most companies embarking on exporting decide to engage in some form of direct exporting. There are four main ways that companies can sell to customers in overseas markets. These are:

- **selling direct from your home base;**
- **setting up an overseas operation;**
- **using a sales agent in the target market;**
- **using a distributor in the target market.**

Selling direct

Selling direct from your home base is an easy way to start selling into overseas markets. You can start by using your existing sales team or you can start by using your website. You can of course develop a strategy using both your online and offline resources in parallel.

Initially selling direct can be cost-effective, because you can start by using your existing personnel and add resources as you need them. Some of your existing sales team can deal with your overseas customers and you can generate sales by telephone and e-mail, supported by occasional sales visits. You can see how things develop, without making major investments and then decide what other strategies to adopt. You have full control of both the marketing and selling processes. As your export business develops, you can make changes to the way that you market your products and if you decide that some products would be even better suited for overseas markets with modification or further development, this can easily be carried out.

The pros and cons of selling direct

Pros

- You can start by using your existing personnel and add resources as you need them.
- You can see how things develop and then decide what other strategies to adopt.
- You have full control of both the marketing and selling processes.

Cons

- You are a long way from the market.
- You will be responsible for the logistics of shipping your goods.
- You have to manage all the risks of exporting yourself including the risks of possible non-payment of your invoices.
- If the language of your target market is not your own, you will need to consider recruiting a qualified person who speaks that language or provide language training for your staff.

Setting up an overseas operation

Setting up your own operation in an overseas market is the most expensive and time-consuming option for market entry. It is not likely to be the option that you would choose if you are new to exporting and looking at one of your first target markets, but if you are an established exporter and you are prepared to make the investment, it is one of the best methods for a company to get established and achieve rapid growth in a new market. In certain countries you may find restrictions that mean you can only establish a joint venture with a local company or set up a company together with a local businessman.

There are four main ways of establishing your own overseas operation:

- Set up a local office.
- Set up a subsidiary company.
- Purchase a local company.
- Establish a joint venture.

The pros and cons of setting up your own operation

Pros

- Your local presence means that you are well placed to identify and exploit opportunities.
- You have control of your operations.
- You keep all of the profits from your operations.
- You can plan for the long term.
- You can expand or contract your operations if the local situation changes.
- Your customers will see you as a local supplier.
- You can provide the level of after-sales service that your products require.
- If things go wrong a locally established subsidiary company limits your liability.
- If you set up a joint venture, you share the profits, but on the other hand you also share the risks. You also get the benefit of your partner's local knowledge.

Cons

- The financial cost of setting up a local operation is high.
- You will need professional advice on the legal and financial ramifications and requirements.
- A local operation will require greater resources to set up, manage and operate than alternative methods of market entry.
- If you don't use a local partner, you take on all the risks yourself.
- It can be costly and difficult to extract yourself if things do not work out. This is particularly the case with a joint venture.

Using a sales agent

A sales agent acts on behalf of your company by introducing you to customers and helping you to obtain orders from them. They are sometimes called commission agents, because they are paid a commission on any sales that they make. The level of commission varies and it is usually only paid once the order is complete, the goods have been shipped and paid for. A good sales agent gives you a high degree of local knowledge and because he is only paid his commission once you have been paid, he has a vested interest in making sure that you get paid. In choosing a sales agent, you need to satisfy yourself about their market knowledge and the level of contacts that they have in your target industries. Make sure that they have experience of selling your type of product, ask for references and examine their client list. Make sure that you get good legal advice before setting up an agency contract.

The pros and cons of using a sales agent

Pros

- The right agent will be able to identify and exploit opportunities.
- They should already have good relationships with the buyers at key potential customers.
- This means they should be productive from the start, whereas setting up your own arrangements would take time.
- You avoid the costs of using your own employees in the marketplace on a day-to-day basis, although you will still need to train the agent and support him with regular visits.
- Using an agent gives you greater control over things like price and conditions than if you were using a distributor.
- You can control your brand and how it is used much more than you could if you were operating through a distributor.
- Based on their experience an agent can give you advice on the creditworthiness of a particular customer.

Cons

- You still have to manage shipments from your works to the end customer, including paperwork and customs clearance formalities.
- You need to specify in the agent's contract what matters they will deal with on your behalf.
- If you want them to carry out proper credit checks on customers locally, you will need to include that in the contract and the commission structure will need to reflect the costs of this.

- Since the agent will be the main contact with your customers in the target market, you will certainly lose some control over marketing and your brand image.
- Most agents will not handle after-sales service as well as you would yourself, since they have already been paid their commission on the supply contract.

Using a distributor

The difference between a distributor and a sales agent is that a sales agent finds you customers, whereas a distributor is your customer. A distributor buys goods from you and resells them in the overseas market. Depending on your type of product, many distributors will also hold stock of your product (or at least of spare parts and consumables) at their premises to support your customers in the market. In this way an overseas distributor operates in much the same way as a distributor would in your home market.

As with sales agents, you should do your homework and make sure that the distributor has experience of selling your type of product and has existing customers for the type of product that you sell. It is also very important to make sure that they do not sell products that compete directly or indirectly with your own. Distribution law is complex and you should make sure that you get good legal advice before setting up a distributorship agreement.

The pros and cons of using a distributor

Pros

- A distributor takes on all of the logistics problems of getting your goods to the customer in your target overseas market.
- A distributor takes over many of the trade-related risks, including supplying credit and getting paid locally.
- An established distributor will already have a list of contacts to whom he can introduce your products.
- An established distributor can use his reputation to support the introduction of your brand into the market.

- Distributors will take over the marketing and sales promotion functions for your products in the overseas market including producing sales literature in their own language, carrying out advertising and taking part in exhibitions. They will probably expect some financial contribution from you to support some of these activities.
- Most distributors keep stock of the products that they sell. Depending on your type of product the stock may be complete items or just spare parts.

Cons

- Distributors will expect large discounts on the products they buy from you.
- They will also expect more extended payment terms than you would offer in your domestic market.
- The customers become *their* customers and not yours. Most distributors keep their customer lists to themselves.
- Distributors add their own mark-up, so you lose any control over the selling price for your products in the target market place.
- If the selling price they set is too high and inhibits sales growth, they will probably ask for a larger discount rather than reducing their own margin.
- Distributors may rebrand your product, sell it under their own name or change the brand image from the image that you have developed in your home market.
- Distributors will usually demand a long period of exclusivity and you need to make sure that you have adequate safeguards in place to allow you to part company if they clearly do not perform.

Deciding which entry strategy to use

Exporting will generate additional sales for your company, but you will need to handle paperwork, shipping, customs clearance, warehousing and after-sales service and you will have additional legal, financial and accounting requirements to those that you would have to deal with in your domestic market. Selling directly gives you overall control of your operations, but it also brings with it all of the costs. Although you have less control when you use an intermediary, they will handle the importation, paperwork, warehousing and shipping of your goods to the end customers.

In deciding which entry strategy is right for you, you should consider the following:

- **Do you have the necessary skills, including the language ability, to make contacts and generate sales?**
- **Do you have the necessary time and does your company have the financial resources to set up and manage a local office or subsidiary?**
- **Are there local restrictions that would limit the way you can operate in your target market? In some countries only a national can own a company. In others you need a local partner or have to form a joint venture with a local company.**
- **What are the usual distribution channels for products like yours in your target market?**
- **Are your key competitors present in your target market and, if so, how do they operate?**
- **Are your products of a standard type that lends itself to warehousing and distribution or are they custom-made depending on the technical requirements of the customer?**
- **Does your product require specialist after-sales support that would need to be provided by your own company? If so, direct sales, even if supported by a local agent, would be more appropriate than selling through a distributor.**

You also need to decide whether it is more important for you to keep costs down to a minimum or to have control of the selling process. Remember that an intermediary will have its own priorities, which may or may not always be the same as yours.

Marketing channels

The things that you require from distribution in an export market are the same as those that you would require from distribution in your home market. Distribution involves:

- **marketing channels;**
- **physical distribution;**
- **customer service.**

The main difference is that in export markets you expect your local presence, whether it is a distributor or your own entity, to have the local channels to market, and you also expect them to handle the physical distribution of your goods to the customer and the customer service function.

The marketing channels that can be used for exporting are the same as those that can be used in your domestic market. The difference is that in your domestic market you will control how you use these channels, but in export markets some of them will be used by your distributor. Potential customers may still look at your website, but they will also look at your distributor's website, and it will be the distributor that uses e-marketing and direct mail. Figure 5.2 shows the range of marketing channels that are available to you in most markets.

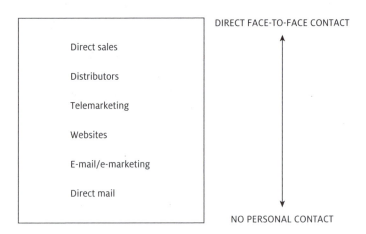

DIRECT FACE-TO-FACE CONTACT

Direct sales

Distributors

Telemarketing

Websites

E-mail/e-marketing

Direct mail

NO PERSONAL CONTACT

Figure 5.2   Marketing channels

As with most things in exporting, there is no 'one size fits all'. If you decide to set up your own company in a particular export market, the available channels to market will be similar to those available in your own country. If you decide to use distribution, the available channels to market will usually be as shown in Figures 5.3 for indirect selling or 5.4 for direct selling.

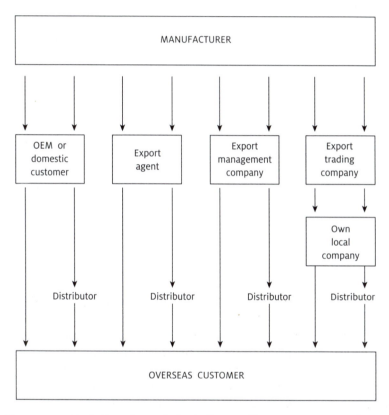

Figure 5.3   Marketing channels for indirect selling to overseas markets

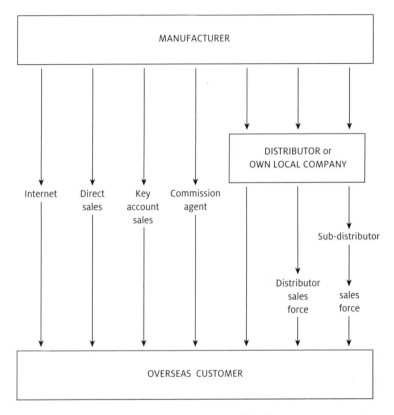

Figure 5.4 Marketing channels for direct selling into overseas markets

Exporting services is different from selling manufactured goods overseas, because normally there is no actual product on the shelf. There may be a standard product as in the case of items such as media products or software, but hard copies of these products are likely to be produced locally in the overseas market by a local company, a franchise holder or a local distributor. Marketing channels for selling services overseas are shown in Figure 5.5.

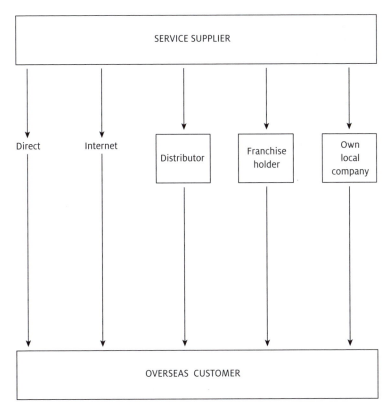

Figure 5.5 Marketing channels for selling services to overseas markets

6

Working through sales agents and distributors

Because it is not easy to manage overseas business at a distance, most exporters decide to set up a local presence in some or all of their target markets. The most common approach is to use a local distributor or agent. Before we look at how you find and select agents and distributors we need to examine the differences between the two types of operation and how they compare. The most important thing to understand is that essentially a sales agent finds you customers, whereas a distributor is your customer.

Agent	Distributor
An agent does not buy the goods from the supplier (principal) and never owns the goods.	A distributor purchases products from the supplier (principal) and owns the goods.

Agent	Distributor
An agent finds customers for the principal and is paid a commission. The supplier invoices the end customer.	A distributor adds his/her profit and resells the goods.
The supplier determines the selling prices and the terms of sale.	A distributor determines the selling prices and the terms of sale.
The supplier knows the identity of the end customer.	The supplier does not usually know the identity of the end customer.

The type of product that you are selling and the nature of your business will determine whether you should be looking for an agent or a distributor. A company bidding for infrequent, high-value contracts would probably use an agent. A company selling a product that needed a local supply of spare parts would probably decide to use a distributor.

Typical characteristics of business through a distributor or an agent

	Distributor	Agent
Order value is:	low	high
Order frequency is:	high	low
Local margin is:	high	low
Local stocking:	yes	no
Control of pricing by principal:	no	yes

Finding and selecting overseas agents and distributors

The key to success in selling through distributors or sales agents is to do your research properly. You need to make sure that you select a distributor or agent with good market knowledge that is fully qualified to sell your type of product, that has a good existing customer base and that can show a good track record of selling similar types of products. As a rule of thumb, where possible you need to find and research enough companies to be able to make a final shortlist of at least three. It is also very important to select a distributor or agent that you feel comfortable with and can work closely with on a personal basis.

How to set about finding an agent or distributor

There are many organisations that can help you to find representation in your target market. In most major exporting countries, these include government organisations as well as commercial companies. You should consider any or all of the following:

- **Your local contact at the government organisation that provides support to exporters.**
- **Word of mouth. Your existing business contacts can also help. If you already do business with one or two customers in your target market, ask them who they like to deal with locally. If you have contacts in other companies with similar or complementary (but not competing) products that have been successful in your target market, ask them for recommendations. If you have a successful distributor in a neighbouring market, ask them what they think; for example, if you have a successful distributor in Australia they may be able to recommend some companies in New Zealand.**
- **Trade associations. Contact your local trade association. You can find details of trade associations for your industry from the Trade Association Forum,** www.taforum.org.

- The internet. Do a search on the internet for 'Export Agents' and 'Export consultants'.
- UK Exporters Ltd. This is an independent company that runs the British Exporters' website, www.exportuk.co.uk. It offers a range of subscription services including an 'Agents wanted' service.
- Yellow Pages, www.yell.com or the business-to-business search engine Kompass, www.kompass.co.uk. (They cover 60 countries worldwide.)
- Your local Chamber of Commerce.
- An organisation set up to encourage trade between your country and your target market. For Indian companies wanting to trade with the UK or UK companies wanting to trade with India, this would be the UK India Business Council (UKIBC), www.ukibc.com. The UKIBC works closely with UKTI.
- A commercial organisation that specialises in helping companies to find suitable representation in specific markets. Examples include Foreign Market Consulting, www.fmcon.com, for Turkey and One Agenda, www.one-agenda.co.uk, for countries in central and Eastern Europe.
- Major banks.
- Taking part in an exhibition in your target market.
- Taking part in a trade mission to your target market.

Overseas Market Introduction Service (OMIS)

Of particular interest to UK exporters is the Overseas Market Introduction Service (OMIS) offered by UKTI. For a competitive fee, you can commission research through UKTI into a particular market. This can include preparation of a list of potential distributors in the country and even help in setting up meetings with these potential distributors. OMIS uses the services of the UKTI trade teams located in the British embassies, high commissions and consulates across the world. Using their local staff means that you have access to their local language skills, market knowledge and commercial and political contacts.

The key factors to consider when choosing an agent or distributor

The key factors to consider when selecting a distributor or agent to represent you in a particular overseas market are:

- Are they well established in your target market?
- Do they have a good reputation with key customers and potential customers?
- How do they compare with their main competitors?
- Are they located in the market's major business centre?
- Do they have good coverage of the rest of the market?
- What product lines do they have?
- Will your product fit in well with their existing product portfolio?
- Do they sell any competing lines?
- Do they have a good and experienced sales team?
- Do their salespeople have experience of selling your type of product?
- Do they have experience of selling to your target industries?
- Is their sales team well managed, with incentive schemes based on achievement?
- Are you confident that they can provide you with realistic sales forecasts to feed into your budgeting?
- Do they employ people who can deal with you in your own language? (It is important that they have people who can manage your day-to-day business in your own language and it is not just the owner or managing director who speaks it.)
- Do they have the warehousing, servicing and other facilities that you require for your products?
- Do they have a good credit rating? You should use a company such as Dun & Bradstreet to carry out credit checks on the companies that you shortlist. The report you get will also tell you what sort of credit limit other suppliers give them and what their payment record is.

Agent/distributor questionnaire

A good way to make sure that you ask all the right questions and get them answered is to prepare an agent/distributor questionnaire and to get the prospective agents/distributors that you are evaluating to complete it for you. An example of such a questionnaire is shown below.

Agent/distributor questionnaire

Please answer all questions as fully as possible. Attach your company brochure, sample sales literature, financial statements and any other material that you think would be helpful to us in evaluating your company.

Full Company Name:

Address:

Tel No:
Contact e-mail address:
Date your company was established:
Name of Chief Executive:
Name and position of the person completing this form:

Number of employees:
Annual company turnover:
Please give a brief description of your company business:

Please list the main product lines that you sell:

Please indicate the main industries that you sell to:

Please detail the geographical area that you cover:

Please give the locations of any regional sales offices or field sales personnel that you have:

Do you have experience of selling XYZ type of equipment?
Yes ☐   No ☐

If yes, what brand(s) did you sell:

What was the annual turnover that you achieved:

What do you estimate as the size of the market in your territory for XYZ products (in €m per year):

What share of that market do you believe you can achieve for us (as a percentage market share and as annual sales in €k):

How would your company plan to promote and sell our products:

What information can you provide on the main competitors for XYZ product (companies, brands, distributors, market share):

Please supply details of your banks and other financial references:

Date:
Authorised signature:

Legal aspects of dealing with agents and distributors

The laws relating to setting up and dealing with agents and distributors are complex and difficult for a layman to understand. For that reason I would strongly recommend that before you start to work with overseas agents and/or distributors you consult a specialist lawyer to get some broad guidelines, and then use the same company to help you to draft out standard agency and distribution agreements.

The key to dealing with any agent or distributor is to do your homework and make sure that you feel comfortable working with them. Working with an agent or distributor is like a marriage. It requires give and take on both sides and divorce can become both vitriolic and expensive. Some companies only start to look at the small print of their agreements when things go wrong, but by then it is too late.

In general terms, agency law is more onerous than distribution law with regard to termination and compensation, but distribution is covered by detailed competition laws, whereas 'genuine agents' are not.

Within the UK the key EU directives and applicable laws are:

Agents:
> EU Directive 86/653 (18th December 1986)
> The Commercial Agents (Council Directive) Regulations 1993

Distributors:
> Articles 81–82 EC
> The Competition Act (1998)

The EU directive on agency agreements covers all EU countries, but the local legislation, often with local interpretations, varies from country to country. Although these laws only apply to EU countries, many other countries around the world have similar legislation.

In most countries distribution law is more evenly balanced than agency law (which tends to favour the agent). If you decide to sell through agents you need to use a clear legal agreement to control territory, product range, pricing, targets, reporting requirements, negotiating limits and commission rates.

If you decide to sell through distributors you should use your agreement to specify your prices and discounts to them, the products included, the area of exclusivity, the period of the appointment, termination arrangements, the obligations and reporting requirements of the distributor, the obligations of the principal, and the situation with regard to sales by the principal.

As indicated above, the one area where distribution law is more complicated than agency law is in the area of complying with unfair competition legislation. Article 81(1) EC and member states' national law equivalents prohibit agreements that affect trade between EU member states and that have an anti-competitive object or effect. In particular they prohibit agreements that fix prices or other trading conditions, limit production or share markets. The distinction between agency and distribution is key in the application of EU competition laws. The rules don't apply where a principal uses a 'genuine agent'. Under EU law, to be considered 'genuine', agents must bear little or no financial or commercial risk in relation to the activities for which they have been appointed. This means that they must just be acting on the principal's behalf and must not be exposed to contractual risks with the customers or be required to purchase and hold stock from the principal for resale to the customers.

Competition law affects all trade within the EU and EEA (European Economic Area) and similar legislation affects the United States. If you are a supplier with less than 15 per cent market share you are unlikely to breach the act. If you have a significant market share you should take professional advice and use block exemptions in exclusive agreements.

If you are a supplier, you must not:

- **dictate the prices charged by your distributors;**
- **impose unfair purchase conditions;**
- **apply different conditions or prices to similar transactions (with the same or with different distributors);**
- **restrict who your distributors can buy from;**
- **restrict who your distributors can supply to;**
- **act to limit competition in the market;**
- **limit production or markets to the consumer's detriment.**

Distributors should not:

- **collaborate with others to fix prices or limit competition;**
- **promote products outside the area covered by their agreement with the supplier.**

Agency and distributor contracts

Once you have decided on the agent or distributor that you want to work with in your target market, it is important to prepare and conclude an agreement with them. The agreement should be a clear and detailed written contract covering all of the key points that will be important to your working relationship.

Again, I would strongly recommend that you get proper legal advice with regard to the preparation of both agency and distributorship agreements. This means not just using your existing company lawyer, but using a law company that specialises in international contract law. They may be expensive, but you will only need to use them to work with you to prepare a standardised contract. Once you have this you can use it for all of your future agency and distributorship agreements.

Managing distributors

Day-to-day management

A good distributor will have a number of key product ranges – often as many as six. Ideally, you want to be sure that your product range is one of their top ranges, but you have to accept that the same salespeople who sell your product range will be putting in time selling other companies' products. If you try to support the business from your office with just phone calls and e-mails, you should not be surprised to find that other companies' products are getting more sales time. To manage a distributor properly you need to visit them regularly, both to review progress and to give support where needed. If your product is technical in nature, you may need to make joint visits to key potential customers.

Promotional and presentation material

If the language in your target market is not your own, there is little point in providing end customers with sales material and presentations in your own language. They will need to have these materials in their own language. If you are going to carry out training of your distributor's sales team, the material you will be using needs to be sent out to the distributor prior to the training so that it can be translated into the local language. It is also useful if you or your distributor can do some work ahead of the training to establish the size of the market in their area/country and the key potential customers.

Overseas distributor meetings or conferences

An overseas distributor conference is similar to a sales conference, but involves a company's overseas distribution. It has much the same aims as a management conference, but with the emphasis on sales and growing them. The delegates would normally be the key sales and management personnel from a company's major overseas distributors. The number of delegates would probably be between 20 and 50, depending on the number of distributors that you have.

Distributor conferences are often organised to take place in the spring or early summer – before the holiday season starts. The results and agreed targets resulting from the conference can then be fed into your company budgeting process in the autumn. Typically a distributor conference would last two to three days.

7

Sales promotion

Sales promotion includes such things as websites, sales literature, presentations, advertising, exhibitions and trade visits. It is an essential sales tool in any market and is just as important for export markets as for your domestic market. When planning your sales promotional activities for overseas markets, it is important to bear in mind that each market is different. This means that some sales promotional activities are better suited to some markets than others, and even the same activity may need to be modified or varied to suit the requirements of different markets or to take into account different languages and cultures.

Understanding your target market

For each of your target markets you need to understand who your potential customers are, the factors that motivate them to buy, and how you can get your products in front of them. You need to understand the methods of sales promotion that are used locally, since these may be different from those used in your domestic market or may be used in ways that reflect a distinctive local culture. You also need to find out how established competitors operate in the market and the methods of sales promotion that they use. To get information on all of these things, you need to carefully research the market and use the results from this research to help plan your approach to sales promotion.

As a minimum you need to find out the following for each of your target markets:

- **What are the main methods of communication used? Press, TV, internet, e-mail, direct mail?**
- **What methods of sales promotion are used?**
- **What marketing tools are currently used?**
- **What cultural issues could affect marketing or sales promotion?**
- **Who are the potential customers?**
- **What motivates them to buy?**
- **What are the best ways to reach potential customers in this market?**
- **Who are the main competitors?**
- **How do these competitors operate?**
- **What media methods do they use?**
- **What is the level of their advertising and sales promotion?**
- **Do they have a local website in the local language?**
- **Can you obtain copies of the major competitors' brochures, data sheets and other presentational material?**

Refining your positioning, your product and image

Because every market is different you may need to modify your product, or modify the way that you position your product for a new target market. The way that you position your product will reflect the different requirements and preferences of your potential customers and the way that the market works. This will have a direct impact on the way that you promote your product in the marketplace.

You need to consider:

- **the product price or pricing structure;**
- **how customers will buy it;**
- **why customers will buy it;**
- **how to handle sales;**
- **how to handle customer service.**

In your domestic market you may use the image of your company as a reliable supplier with local support and service just round the corner to help you to sell your product. In an overseas market you would be reliant on your distributor to develop the same image. This may or may not be possible and you may decide to use a different image and promote your product in the target market as a robust and well-engineered product or a state-of-the-art ultra-modern product.

Your market positioning for your target market needs to take into account local customer expectations, market trends, your product and company image, product suitability, packaging requirements, distribution channels and local competition. All of this is important in deciding how you will sell and promote your product and the level of pricing that you will adopt.

Reviewing your sales promotion for overseas markets

If you are already successful in your domestic market, you will already have a range of promotional materials at your disposal. Some of these may be suitable for use in overseas markets, but most will need some modification or even a complete revamp. If you want to get the best out of your sales promotional materials for export markets, I would recommend that you get them reviewed by an export communications consultant. Many overseas government organisations offer such support to their exporters. The Export Communications Review (ECR), which is available to UK exporters, is one of the best schemes of this kind.

The Export Communications Review (ECR)

The ECR offers companies impartial and objective advice on language and cultural issues in order to help them develop an effective communications strategy for existing and future export markets. The scheme is offered by UK Trade & Investment and managed by the British Chambers of Commerce. The reviews are carried out by accredited export communications consultants, who have been trained in the discipline of export communications by the British Chambers of Commerce. All of the

ECR consultants are multi-skilled, have experience in exporting and international marketing, are linguists, and have lived and worked abroad. They discuss how a company tackles (or plans to tackle) the language and cultural issues that arise when trading overseas. They can identify communication strengths and weaknesses and offer unbiased objective advice.

The consultants can review all written and spoken communications with a specific overseas market, or they can focus on a company's specific export activity, such as:

- **press releases and promotional materials, technical documentation and manuals, catalogues and packaging for international audiences;**
- **preparation for and representation at an overseas trade show or exhibition;**
- **preparation for a presentation to an international audience;**
- **improving relationships with overseas agents and distributors;**
- **international sales and invoicing processes;**
- **systems for handling foreign phone calls and e-mails;**
- **training of overseas staff;**
- **language training needs in the UK;**
- **recruitment of export staff;**
- **international website strategy.**

The consultant provides the company with a customised written report that includes practical recommendations and information on possible suppliers and costs.

Websites

As well as providing companies with a major sales channel for all types of products, the internet has become the main channel for customers and potential customers to find out about companies and their products. This makes your company's website a key support tool for your export drive. Having said that, you should be aware that the development and use of the internet and access to high-speed broadband networks is still not uniform around the globe. When you look at developing countries, even getting access to the internet is not as easy as in the United States, Europe and Australasia. Not every country has the broadband access and speeds that South Korea has.

If you intend to expand your business into major countries where your own language is not commonly spoken, you need to consider developing your website so that it can be accessed and used in other languages. This is not easy and it is obviously also more expensive than developing and maintaining a website in just one language.

The best way to decide what changes you need to make to your website is to have it reviewed by an export communications consultant. A website review should involve a comprehensive analysis of your website, covering:

- **the technical aspects involved in setting up an international website;**
- **the optimum design, structure and navigation of the site for overseas visitors;**
- **inclusion of appropriate international content;**
- **translation and localisation for target export markets;**
- **promotion of the site in overseas markets, including a 'localised' approach to search engine optimisation;**
- **monitoring the site's performance;**
- **managing the impact of a successful site.**

Sales literature

For your domestic market you will have a range of sales literature available. Depending on your type of product, this will probably include a corporate brochure, sales brochures, leaflets and possibly also datasheets. These will all be available in your own language. So what should you do for overseas markets where the local language is different? What should you prepare and how should you go about it?

My suggestion is to look at the preparation of foreign-language material cautiously. If your target market is Brazil, but you haven't even made a first visit to the market, don't get all of your sales literature translated into Portuguese before you start. If you have already made several visits to the market and have just appointed a distributor there, then the situation is somewhat different.

For any target market where your own language is not spoken I would suggest that you adopt a two-stage approach to producing any of your literature in a foreign language.

Introductory leaflet

Stage one is material that you need in order to make your initial entry into your target market and to find effective distribution. You cannot assume that the key decision makers at major customers or potential distributors will fully understand the information that you provide about your company and its products if it is not written in their own language.

I have found that for market entry what you really need is a high-quality two-sided single-page leaflet with one side printed in your own language and the other side giving exactly the same information in the language of your target market. The leaflet should include details of your company, your products and the applications that your products could be used for.

Product and other literature

Once you have appointed a local distributor in your target market and its salespeople are starting to make customer visits, they need to have some support material printed in their own language. This does not need to be all of your sales leaflets and data sheets, but does need to cover key products that they want to discuss with end customers. You need to make the files containing these key sales leaflets and data sheets available to the distributor, so that it can use either its own qualified staff or a local agency to produce versions of these in their own language.

Presentations

Presentations make very effective sales tools. When you are selling overseas, your sales presentations can be easily modified by your local distributor for use by its own sales force. If the local language is different from yours, the distributor can translate the text of the presentations for you. Simplicity is important in presentations and you want to make sure that the main features and benefits of your products are clear to see.

Some tips when preparing and making a presentation

- Use large font sizes for the text.
- Use an easy-to-read typeface such as Times New Roman or Arial.
- Don't try to get too many lines of text on a slide – about 10 is ideal.
- Use introductory slides with key headings and follow these up with separate slides expanding each of these headings.
- Bring bullet points in one by one to avoid the audience trying to read the whole slide rather than listening to your presentation.
- Consider using a background colour to enhance the impact of your presentation.
- Prepare a 'slide master' or 'background template' with your company name and logo on it.
- Include horizontal lines top and bottom to give your slides an 'active area'.
- Enhance your presentation by importing tables or graphs from Microsoft Excel (if applicable).
- Import suitable photos into your slides (if applicable).
- You can copy an open web page onto a PowerPoint slide by pressing the 'Control' (ctrl) and 'Print Screen' (PrtSc) buttons together and then using the 'edit' and 'paste' functions in Powerpoint.

Advertising

The level of advertising that you will use in your target market will depend on your type of product and the way that you are distributing it. If it is a consumer product then levels of advertising would probably need to be similar to those in your domestic market. If you are selling industrial products or capital goods, your advertising is likely to be more specific and targeted around things like product launches or major exhibitions.

When you are planning to advertise in overseas markets it is important to discuss your advertising campaign with your local agent or distributor. Local agents or distributors may be prepared to fund and manage advertising themselves, but more often than not they will expect you to fund part, if not all, of the cost. It is important to use their local knowledge to make sure that your advertising is tailored to the market, uses the appropriate messages and is in the local language. You may decide that it would be more effective to combine the advertising of your product with your distributor's own advertising programme.

Exhibitions and trade shows

Exhibitions and trade shows are important promotional tools and can be good showcases for your products. With regard to overseas markets, taking part in an exhibition can be a good way of taking a first step into the market. It gives you the opportunity:

- **to meet customers face to face;**
- **to demonstrate your products;**
- **to find out what customers in your target market really want;**
- **to meet with potential distributors/agents;**
- **to see who your competitors are and what products they are offering in this market.**

One of the main advantages is that there will be a large number of potential customers concentrated in one place. Also, if you exhibit as part of a country group you have the opportunity to network and to gain from the experience of other, more experienced exhibitors from your own country.

You need to select your exhibition carefully. Ideally you want to take part in an exhibition that is specific to your type of industry or product and not just a 'general' trade fair, where most of the visitors will be ordinary members of the public and not potential customers. As with any exhibition, you need to have a plan and decide what you want to achieve from it.

If it is your first time exhibiting in the country your goals may be:

- **to meet with and evaluate the three distributors on your short-list;**
- **to meet with potential customers and find out what they really want from your product;**
- **to assess the competition and their products;**
- **to see what new products or technologies are on offer;**
- **to network with other exhibitors from your country.**

Most major countries offer support to their exporters, and this usually includes either financial or material support for taking part in overseas exhibitions and trade shows. Many international exhibitions have country 'pavilions', and at the Hanover Fair in Germany, for example, there will be a US Pavilion, an Indian Pavilion, a South African Pavilion and many more. At a major event such as the Shanghai International Trade Fair a country pavilion would probably be an individual structure, but at many events, it would be a grouping of stands in one section of an exhibition hall. The pavilion would include the stands of a large number of exhibitors from that country, together with a support stand from the government support organisation.

Sector-focused trade missions/visits

Trade missions are organised visits to target markets. They usually last between three and eight days and are often specific to a particular industry or event. They offer companies an excellent opportunity to research overseas markets. They can also be used to generate business opportunities, meet potential distributors or agents or assess possible sales and promotion strategies. They are an ideal way to visit a market that you are unfamiliar with, and you can gain from the experience of the mission leader and others on the mission as well as from the local contacts that you make. I would strongly recommend a trade mission to make initial exploratory visits to complex countries such as Russia, Japan, China or Brazil. To make the most of a trade visit you need to set clear objectives of what you want to achieve from it and you should always take appropriate product literature with you, translated into the local language.

Support may be available from your government to help you organise and make the most of trade visits. In the UK, small businesses taking part in these trade missions are eligible for travel grants to cover up to half the cost of the visit. The process works in a similar way to exhibition support and is often managed by a Chamber of Commerce on behalf of UKTI. In the US, the US Commercial Service organises trade missions.

The internet as a sales channel

The internet offers significant advantages to all companies wanting to do business internationally. The scope and depth of a website is determined by the range and diversity of a company's products, not by the size of the company. Small companies can have a website that is as good and comprehensive as those of their larger competitors and can give the impression of being large and knowledgeable. Another advantage of using the internet to develop your international sales is that if a company is doing its selling, marketing and advertising online, it can avoid some of the costs that it would have to incur in developing international sales by traditional methods.

Websites for international e-commerce

If your company is well promoted and your website attracts attention from search engines, there is no reason why you cannot pick up some business from anywhere in the world. In this way your company's website can be a key support tool for your export drive. However, you need to understand that you cannot handle overseas business on your website in exactly the same way that you handle domestic sales. Even if the requirements for order handling and after-sales service for export business are similar whether you are dealing with them on- or offline, there are additional national and international regulations relating to e-commerce.

Types of site

Ordinary website or e-commerce site?

A website needs to be well constructed and easy to navigate so that customers will use it and will come back to it. Not all companies need to take orders on their website and not every company needs to have a truly transactional e-commerce site. Many companies selling overseas just use their website to provide potential customers with information about the company and its products, not to actually transact business on the site. Other companies need to be able to provide individual quotations for jobs or projects; although the details of the enquiry can be taken on the website through the 'contact us' page, a separate quotation would then need to be prepared and e-mailed to the customer. But if your product is easy to store, pack and despatch, it is likely to benefit if you have an e-commerce site.

Domain names

Your domain name is the title and address of your website. Most website owners try to buy a domain name that says something about their business or what their site does, or one that incorporates their main brand or company name.

A domain name is the first part of the web address after www. that is entered into a web browser to find a web page on the internet. (It is also the part after the @ sign in an e-mail address.) So in the web address **www.mycompany.com**, 'mycompany' is the domain name. In selecting a domain name exporters need to consider a number of things. The name needs to be short, simple and, most importantly, memorable for potential customers in the target markets.

The second part of the address, '.com', is called the TLD (Top Level Domain). For international business it is best if you can get the TLD

'.com' or failing that '.co' or '.eu' (for European Union) for your main website. But it is also useful if you can purchase the local country codes – '.co.uk', '.fr' or '.au', for example – for the individual local markets that you intend to trade in. A local country domain name can increase local brand awareness and brand loyalty. It can also help you to increase your search engine ranking on search engines that are popular in your target market. If you only intend to have one website, you can still own local domain names and arrange to redirect users to your main website.

Make your website user-friendly for foreign visitors

If you already have a website and want to use it for international trade, it makes sense to get an export communications consultant to carry out a review of your website. They can advise you of changes that you can make to your website to make it more user-friendly to overseas customers. They can also help you to develop a website specifically for international trade. An international website needs to be designed and set up in such a way that the structure and navigation are simple for overseas visitors. You need to make sure that the language used in your website is clear and understandable to people whose mother tongue is not your own. Avoid the use of unexplained jargon or unnecessarily complicated language. You need to make sure that you include an appropriate amount of international content.

If you intend to expand your business into major countries where your own language is not commonly spoken, you need to consider developing a website in the local language.

Web hosting

A web hosting service is a type of internet hosting service that allows individuals and companies to make their own website accessible via the world wide web. Web hosts are companies that provide space on a server they own or lease for use by their clients as well as providing internet connectivity, typically in a data centre. In recent years companies, large and small, have turned to web hosting companies rather than using their own IT resources. The hosting companies have large banks of computers, which will store all of your information for a monthly fee. Also, they are able to handle large amounts of traffic, which significantly reduces the possibility of your website crashing. This is particularly important if you are using your website for international business, where different time zones mean that the pattern of people accessing your website will be different from that expected just from your domestic market. The companies offer better protection for your information as well as better protection from crashes, and at the same time you can save money on equipment and staff. Most companies select a web host based in their own country, but in some circumstances there can be advantages in using a host based in the target market itself.

E-commerce sites

Setting up a site

If you want to sell online rather than use your website just to provide information on your company and products to your international customers, you need to have an e-commerce site. As with an ordinary website, the options with an e-commerce site are to buy a package from a web hosting company or to have one built for you by a web design company. With the additional factors necessary to conduct overseas trade, most companies that want to use the site to export their product choose to have it built for them by experts.

Web analytics

Web analytics software allows companies to track which pages of their website are most popular, which promotions are clicked on most – basically which parts and which products seem to attract users and which parts don't. It allows you to monitor traffic to your website in real time. You can track where users enter and where they leave, where they come from (which search engines, etc) and where they go next, how long they stay on the site and how many pages they look at while they are there. You can log the number of daily visitors and where in the world they are all located. This allows you to make comparisons between domestic and overseas visitors to your site and to understand whether your site is as easy to navigate and understand for an overseas visitor as for a domestic one.

Search engine rankings

The huge increase in the number of companies operating and selling on the internet has dramatically increased the competition between companies to get visitors to their websites rather than to those of their competitors. When carrying out a web search, most people will only look at the first page of search results and often only at the top two or three results. So making sure that your site gets high up in the results is important to the success of your website, and search engine rankings are just as important for attracting overseas customers as domestic ones. Good rankings mean success and you can improve your search engine ranking by using search engine optimisation (SEO). If you have decided to set up a website in your target market, or to use a local domain name, you may need to get specialist SEO advice from an export communications expert. This is because many local search engines filter the search results in such a way that they only display local country domains. You would also need to make sure that you are registered with search engines that are popular in your target market.

Getting paid

Fortunately most e-commerce website packages include facilities to make taking orders from overseas easier. As well as accepting credit card payment, most packages include the facility for you to take payment via PayPal or WorldPay or even by electronic funds transfer (EFT). With regard to postage and packing, most e-commerce packages allow you to set up special rates that users can select before they reach checkout. These can include rates for shipment to Europe and the United States, or a facility for the customer to receive a quotation for postage and packing by e-mail.

Online fraud

Online fraud is a potential risk with any online transaction, even when accepting established credit cards issued by major banks. Fraud rates on international online business can be as high as 2 or 3 per cent of business transactions. Companies need to be vigilant and put systems in place to try to weed out transactions that are obviously fraudulent. You can reduce the risks by taking sensible precautions, such as asking the customer to enter the card verification number (CVN). You can also set up your system so that it excludes countries where the risk of credit card fraud is high.

Shipping the goods

The process of shipping goods purchased online is the same as that for shipping goods purchased from you directly. This means that you will have the same types of costs and the same requirements with regard to export regulations, tariffs and taxes, and the same reporting requirements as with orders placed by other means.

Tax requirements

In addition to needing to understand – and state in the terms and conditions on your website – which taxes and tariffs are included in your price, you also need to make yourself aware of any international arrangements that would affect your online business with your target markets. For instance European Union member states tax the sales of goods and services supplied electronically from non-EU companies to customers located in the EU. Non-EU online providers of goods and services are required to register with a tax authority in one of the EU member states, and to collect and remit value added tax (VAT) at the VAT rate of the member state where the customer is located. It is likely that other countries will take a similar approach in the future.

E-commerce regulations

Companies that sell or market products or services online must comply with e-commerce regulations. E-commerce includes selling goods or services over the internet, by e-mail, on interactive digital television or by using mobile phone text messages. All countries have rules and regulations that regulate e-commerce, but if you want to trade online internationally, you need to comply not only with your own national regulations but also with international requirements.

The main international e-commerce regulations are aimed at protecting consumers and sensibly regulating commercial e-mails. The main e-commerce regulations derive from the European Commission (EC) 'Directive 2000/31/EC on electronic commerce', the EC directive 2002/58/EC and the US CAN-SPAM Act of 2003 and their subsequent updates.

The EC Directive 2000/31/EC

As a European Directive, the regulations apply to all European Union member states and affect e-commerce taking place between and within member states. This means that companies in non-EU countries wanting to trade electronically with EU countries also need to take them into account.

The regulations include details of the information that an online service provider must give to a consumer and the limitations on a service provider's liability for unlawful information that they unwittingly carry or store.

The requirements can be divided into three categories: information requirements, commercial requirements and electronic contracting.

Information requirements

These include companies providing their end users with:

- the full name of their business;
- the geographic location;
- contact details, including an e-mail address, to enable direct and rapid communication with their customers;
- details of any relevant trade organisations to which they belong;
- details of any authorisation scheme relevant to their online business;
- their VAT number, if their online activities are subject to VAT;
- a clear indication of prices, if relevant, including any delivery or tax charges.

Commercial communications

Any form of electronic communication (such as e-mail advertising) that is designed to promote goods, services or image, must:

- be clearly identifiable as a commercial communication;
- clearly identify the person and/or organisation on whose behalf it is sent;
- provide clear identification of any promotional offers being advertised, including any discounts, gifts, competitions, games and so on;
- provide a clear explanation of any qualifying conditions regarding such offers;
- provide a clear indication of any unsolicited communications being sent.

Electronic contracting

These requirements apply to anyone who enables end users to place orders online. The company must provide end users with the following information in a 'clear, comprehensive and unambiguous manner' *prior* to an order being placed:

- The company must explain the different technical steps to follow in order to conclude the contract so that end users are made aware of what the process will involve and the point at which they will commit themselves to the contract.
- It must state whether the concluded contract will be filed or not and whether it will be accessible.
- It must have clearly identifiable technical means of identifying and correcting input errors made by an end user prior to placing an order, so that end users know how to correct any mistakes that they make.
- It must state the languages offered for the conclusion of the contract.
- If the company subscribes to any codes of conduct it must supply the details and advise end users how they can access them.
- If you supply end users with terms and conditions applicable to their contract, you must make these available in such a way that

the end user can store and reproduce them: that is, download them onto their computer and subsequently print them out.
- If an end user places an order online, the supplier must acknowledge receipt of the order without delay and by electronic means.
- The supplier must also make available appropriate, effective and accessible technical means that will allow the end user to identify and correct any input errors *prior* to the placing of the order.

Note: These requirements do not apply to transactions between two businesses (ie B2B transactions) if both parties agree to opt out of them.

A company is required to comply with these regulations not just for business within its own country, but even if it is providing its services in a different EU country. The EU also prohibits the transfer of personal data to non-EU countries that do not meet the EU requirements for privacy protection. This means that companies from countries outside the EU wishing to trade online with businesses or consumers within the EU need to be able to prove that they comply with the EU regulations. Some countries, such as the United States, have set up 'safe harbor' agreements with the EU under which their companies can self-certify the fact that they comply with the requirements.

Privacy and Electronic Communications (EC Directive) Regulations 2003

These regulations updated the Telecoms Data Protection Directive in the light of new technologies, and in particular ensured that the privacy rules applicable to phone and fax services should also be applied to e-mail and to the use of the internet. There are four key provisions:

- Anyone who uses cookies (whether they process personal data or not) and similar tracking devices must provide information and offer subscribers or users who are not content to accept them with the chance to refuse.
- The regulations allow for the provision of value added services based on traffic or location data, either by network operators

on their own or in conjunction with third parties. There is no restriction on the type of services that may be provided as long as subscribers give their consent and are informed of the data processing implications.

- They give subscribers the right to decide whether or not they want to be listed in subscriber directories. Subscribers must be given clear information about the directories in question, including any reverse search-type functions, for which additional specific consent is required.
- They require unsolicited commercial e-mail and SMS to individual subscribers to be subject to a prior consent requirement, so that it may only be sent if the recipient has agreed in advance. There is an exception to this rule in the context of an existing customer relationship, where companies may continue to market their own similar products or services on an 'opt-out' basis.

The US CAN-SPAM Act

The CAN-SPAM act covers all commercial messages, including e-mail, that promote content on commercial websites. The original 2003 Act was amended in 2008 and the original four requirements were extended to seven. The main requirements are:

- Don't use false or misleading header information.
- Don't use deceptive subject lines.
- Identify the message as an advertisement.
- Tell recipients where you are located.
- Tell recipients how to opt out of receiving future e-mail from you.
- Honour opt-out requests promptly.
- Monitor what others are doing on your behalf.

You can find out more information about the CAN-SPAM Act on the Federal Trade Commission website, **www.ftc.gov/spam**, including a useful explanatory document entitled 'The CAN-SPAM Act: A compliance guide for business', which can be downloaded as a PDF file.

The key difference between the CAN-SPAM Act and the EU directive is that the EU directive requires prior consent from the recipient before any direct marketing e-mail messages can be sent ('opt-in'), whereas the CAN-SPAM Act allows direct marketing messages to be sent to anyone, without permission, until the recipient explicitly requests that they cease ('opt-out').

Quoting for international business

In principle, quoting for overseas business is not much different from quoting for business in your domestic market. It's just a lot more complicated. When you prepare an export quotation, the packaging requirements will depend on whether the goods are being shipped by road, sea or air, the documentation requirements will depend on the type of product and where you are shipping it to, and there will be a range of different delivery terms (Incoterms) and payment methods available.

Pricing for export business

The most common methods that companies can use to determine their export pricing are cost-plus, top-down and marginal costing. But export pricing is not just determined by analysing your costs and it is important that you understand that cost is only a part of the equation. You also need to take into account the market demand and the competition in your target markets.

Special products and standard products

There are many different types of exporters with many different types of product, but from the point of view of export pricing I would suggest there are two main ways that a company can categorise its products. It can divide its products into 'special' products and 'standard' (or semi-standard) products (some companies will only have one of these two types):

- *Special products.* **Special products may not be considered special by the company that makes them, but by their nature they need to be costed up individually or the price needs to be recalculated due to changes in costs of raw materials or components. So the price of this type of product needs to be calculated for each quotation.**
- *Standard or semi-standard products.* **This type of product covers everything from nuts and bolts to large machines, and from jars of jam to laptop computers. Pricing for this type of product can be set on a regular basis (usually annually) and an export price list prepared.**

In putting together a quotation for a 'special' product, you have to include the usual costs and margins that you would include for your domestic business. Typically, this would be the cost of raw materials, manufacturing and overheads, with your profit margin added. For products that you are selling overseas there would be additional costs and it is quite normal to also add a small additional margin to cover the increased risks and financial costs of international trade.

Companies that are already active in selling overseas have usually prepared their own standard charges that can be added to the quotation for such things as export packing and FOB (free on board) delivery. These sorts of additional charges are usually calculated as a rate per unit of weight or volume, with a minimum charge for items below a certain size. The costs of more specialised types of packaging, additional documentation or certification, and for different delivery terms, would probably need to be calculated by an experienced person such as the shipping manager, who would need to get outside quotations for many of these.

Although all companies quoting for overseas business add their additional costs into their quotations, at the end of the day it is a competitive marketplace and on major projects you will find yourself competing with companies from around the world. This often means that you have to decide whether you can risk being uncompetitive or whether you have to reduce your selling price from the price that you calculate taking into account all your additional costs and your full margin.

Standard products and export price lists

If your product is of the type that lends itself to having a price list, you will probably already have such a list for your domestic market. Price lists make it easier for your sales personnel to put together quotations and can also be used by your overseas distributors to calculate the cost of purchasing goods from you. You can prepare export price lists in your own currency, and convert them to other major currencies if much of your export business will be conducted in those currencies.

If you are just starting to export then deciding on the level of your price list is a decision that will have a profound impact on your ability to develop your export business. Remember that your export price list includes two potential margins. It includes your distributors' margins and, below that, your company's margin, so you often have to be a little creative to ensure that you stay competitive. But remember also that some countries have anti-dumping laws, and if your net selling price appears low you may have to justify it in order to prove that you are not using differential pricing to sell your product unfairly.

Price lists should always give your ex-works prices. This way you know exactly what your margin should be. Remember that if you sell through distributors in your target market, the net price will also include freight costs, customs duties and tariffs, and that once they have added their margin they will also have to add local sales taxes to reach the selling price. It is not unusual for the end-customer selling price in some overseas markets to be 50 per cent higher or even double your normal domestic selling price. But this price level needs to be competitive, if you are to succeed in that market.

Pro forma invoices

Most companies will have a standard format for export quotations that will include details of the products being offered together with details of the packaging, the terms of sale and the payment terms that are being offered. But there is a standard format that is used internationally by overseas customers when they need to apply for an import licence, open a letter of credit or arrange finance for the purchase. This is the pro forma invoice. In most cases the customer will react to your quotation by asking you to send them a pro forma invoice. This usually means that they have decided to accept your offer and need the pro forma invoice to arrange the finance or letter of credit.

A pro forma invoice is a formal document. On the invoice it should clearly state that it is a 'pro forma invoice' and should include a statement saying that it is 'true and correct'. It should also clearly state the country of origin of the goods specified in it. Some countries or banks insist that the pro forma invoice should be authenticated (officially certified as being true and correct) by your local Chamber of Commerce, and some insist that it should also be accompanied by an authenticated certificate of origin. The information that you include on the pro forma invoice is important, not least because, if it is being used to obtain a letter of credit, much of the detail will be included verbatim in the letter of credit itself. The invoice should include:

- the names and addresses of the buyer and the seller;
- the buyer's reference and the date of their enquiry;
- details of the products offered, together with a description of each item;
- the price of each item and the currency (US$, euros, £ sterling, etc);
- the total gross and net shipping weights;
- approximate total volume and dimensions of the consignment when packed for export;
- the delivery point and terms of sale (Incoterms);
- estimated time for delivery;
- terms of payment;
- time that the quotation is valid for.

Keep the above information, and particularly the description of the products offered, simple. Complex language can result in errors in the wording on the letter of credit that is issued.

Export contracts

Having a proper written contract is important when trading internationally. Contracts should be clearly worded and should be in the form of a legal document so that there is no difficulty in interpretation and can be no misunderstanding. They should be prepared for you by a lawyer who is experienced in export contract law and understands your business. For major contracts it is usual to have a standard format of contract into which the key information specific to that contract can be entered. Exporters selling a range of smaller or lower-value products may decide to have a standard quotation format and a separate standard set of 'terms and conditions' that can be attached to every quotation. A written contract should include details of all of the key factors relating to the goods being supplied. This should include, as a minimum, a description of the goods, the price, packing details, trading terms (Incoterms), payment terms and the choice of law, which should make clear the jurisdiction under which arbitration or conciliation would be conducted. The description of the goods should be sufficiently detailed to avoid any dispute between the exporter and the customer, and the detail should be such that the correct commodity classification code can be applied to the goods by customs on arrival.

Payment methods

A major variable in export quotations, particularly when quoting to customers in the developing world, is the method of payment. When you quote in your domestic market, even though you may have some customers on 'advance payment', most of your major customers will probably be on 'open account' with credit terms of 30 days. When selling overseas you have pressure, particularly from creditworthy major customers and distributors, to offer extended credit terms of 60 days or more on open account, and you will have to balance this against the risks of non-payment and the sensible option, in many cases, of insisting on payment in advance or by letter of credit.

The methods of payment most commonly used in international trade are shown in Figure 9.1 and outlined below:

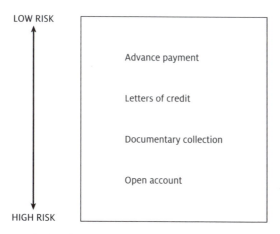

Figure 9.1 Methods of payment used in international trade

- *Advance payment.* **This ensures that payment is cleared before the goods are shipped. The payment is usually made by a SWIFT inter-bank transfer, although for lower-value items it could also be made by credit card payment.**
- *Letters of credit.* **There are different types, but I would strongly recommend that you only accept irrevocable letters of credit that have been confirmed by a bank in your own country. Although a letter of credit is a relatively safe method of payment, you must make sure that all your staff are aware that in order to ensure payment, you must comply strictly with the documentary requirements of the credit. Letters of credit are governed by a set of rules from the International Chambers of Commerce (ICC). The latest version is called Uniform Customs and Practice number 600 (UCP600), and over 90 per cent of the world's banks adhere to the rules in this document.**
- *Documentary collection* **(sometimes called 'cash against documents'). This is raised by the exporter and made out to the customer's bank. It is sent to the customer for acceptance and can be guaranteed by the bank for additional safety.**

- *Open account.* The credit terms can be 30 days, 60 days or even longer, and with 30 days the term may apply from the date of invoice or from the end of the month of invoice, depending on what is specified. As with your domestic business, this type of payment method should only be used for creditworthy customers or distributors who have built up a reliable payment history. Payments should always be made by bank transfer and not by cheque.

Clearly payment in advance is the best and most secure method of payment, and if you are dealing with customers in developed countries it is usual to start working on the basis of advance payment and then to move towards an open account as you build up a trading history. But when dealing with customers in developing countries, the foreign exchange regulations will often not allow money to be paid out overseas until it is clear that goods have actually been shipped. This is why the use of letters of credit is much more widespread with regard to the shipment of goods to developing countries. A letter of credit is an undertaking by a bank to make a payment to a named beneficiary within a specified time, against the presentation of documents that comply strictly with the terms of the letter of credit. A letter of credit provides security to both the exporter and the importer. When you ask for payment by letter of credit, you are transferring the risk of non-payment to the issuing and the confirming banks, so you should understand that they are not going to pay you until they are certain that all the terms of the letter of credit have been met. Thus, if you are going to conduct some of your export business using letters of credit you need to be sure that all personnel who will be involved – sales, finance and logistics personnel – understand the importance of checking the details on the letter of credit and making sure that they comply with them.

Terms of sale (Incoterms)

When quoting to an overseas customer, there needs to be a common understanding of the delivery terms; it is important to use a delivery term that clearly defines where your responsibility for shipment of the goods ends and the customer's responsibility begins. Incoterms (**In**ternational **Co**mmercial **Terms**) are a set of rules for the interpretation of the trade terms that are most commonly used in international trade. They have traditionally been used in international sales contracts where goods pass across national borders. They were first published by the International Chamber of Commerce (ICC), **www.iccwbo.org**, in 1936 and have been updated every 10 years or so since then. The current terms in use are laid down in the 2010 revision, which came into force on 1 January 2011. The basic function of each Incoterm is to clarify how functions, costs and risks are split between the buyer and seller with regard to the delivery of goods as required by a sales contract. Each term clearly specifies the responsibilities of the seller and the buyer; delivery, risks and costs are known at the critical points.

The choice of Incoterm is influenced by the mode of transport that you or your customer chooses. Some terms can be applied to any mode of transport, whereas others apply only to goods shipped by sea. The full rules for using Incoterms are available in the publication 'Incoterms ® 2010', available from the ICC Business Bookstore (**www.iccbooks.com)**.

Incoterms ® 2010 was the first change to Incoterms in 10 years and made some significant changes that reflect changes to the ways that goods are now being shipped. The terms are now split into two Groups (Tables 9.1 and 9.2). Group 1 contains Incoterms applicable to any mode of transport, and Group 2 contains terms that are applicable to sea and inland waterway transport only.

The rules in Table 9.1 can be used for any mode of transport (including cases where a ship is used for part of the carriage). The rules in Table 9.2 apply only to sea freight or inland waterway shipments, where the 'ship's rail' acts as the divider between one term and another. Containerised cargo (even if being shipped by sea) almost always uses the rules shown in Table 9.1, because a container is usually delivered to the carrier.

Clearly the easiest and safest thing for an exporting company to do would be to try where possible to get the safest and most favourable terms of trade that it can. But exporting is a competitive business and it is also important to offer competitive terms to your customers. If you just stick with what is easiest to you, you may find that you lose out and hungrier competitors get the business.

Obviously the mode of transport that you use will limit the Incoterms that you can use. But normal practice also plays its part. In some countries certain terms are taken to be the norm, and if you offer less favourable

Table 9.1 Incoterms applicable to any mode of transport

Group 1. Incoterms applicable to any mode of transport

Incoterm	Description	Transfer of responsibility
EXW	Ex Works	Named place
FCA	Free Carrier	Named place
CPT	Carriage Paid To	Named place of destination
CIP	Carriage and Insurance Paid To	Named place of destination
DAT	Delivered at Terminal	Named place of destination
DAP	Delivered at Place	Named place of destination
DDP	Delivered Duty Paid	Named place of destination

Table 9.2 Incoterms applicable to sea freight shipments only

Group 2. Incoterms applicable to sea and inland waterway transport only

Incoterm	Description	Transfer of responsibility
FAS	Free alongside Ship	Named port of shipment
FOB	Free on Board	Named port of shipment
CFR	Cost and Freight	Named port of shipment
CIF	Cost, Insurance and Freight	Named port of shipment

terms you could lose out. For shipments within the European Union it is standard practice for goods to be sold on a 'delivered' basis.

In its International Trade Guide entitled *Incoterms: An action plan and checklist*, SITPRO provides a checklist to use when deciding which Incoterm to use for shipping to a particular customer. The complete guide can be downloaded from the SITPRO website as a PDF file.

SITPRO's Incoterms checklist

1. What method of transport is to be used?
2. What are the terms currently used? Who chose these?
3. Are there any company policies on which terms should be used and how much responsibility should be taken?
4. Are there any restrictions on the term to be used by the country of importation?
5. Are there any commercial norms in the country with which you are dealing?
6. Discuss the terms to be used with your trading partner – it is important to take their point of view into account.
7. Ensure that both parties understand and can carry out their obligations.
8. Ensure that you are able to obtain enough information to give a quote for a certain Incoterm.
9. Read Incoterms 2010. The introduction gives good advice and can clarify certain issues and the individual terms themselves are accurately described.
10. Ensure all staff (especially those involved in sales and marketing) are properly trained to understand the basic principles of Incoterms, and in particular the details of the individual Incoterms.
11. Incorporate the terms decided into all relevant paperwork such as invoices, quotations, terms and conditions of sale.
12. Review the terms periodically and change them if necessary.

10

Moving your goods

Exporting is not just about finding markets and taking orders. If you don't get your logistics right and goods are delivered late or arrive damaged, you will very quickly lose not only your existing customers, but also other potential customers, who will become aware of your reputation. As well as employing sales personnel who understand export markets, you also need to employ or train up logistics personnel. These personnel need to understand what they can organise themselves, and when they need to use the services of a freight forwarder. You will also need to train personnel in export documentation, the classification of goods and export reporting procedures.

Modes of transport

When you are shipping goods to a particular destination there will usually be a range of available routes and transport methods. Decisions about the mode of transport will be influenced by a number of factors, including the following:

- *The destination.* If the destination is on the same continent and not too far away, then road transport could be the logical choice.

If you are shipping to the other side of the world, the only choice would be by sea or air freight.

- *Availability.* What are transport links like to the country of destination and what modes of transport are readily available?
- *Speed.* How quickly do you need to get your goods to their destination? Are they urgently required (as in the case of emergency spare parts)? Are the goods perishable?
- *Cost.* Obviously there is a difference in cost between different modes of transport.
- *Type of goods.* Are there any special requirements? Are the goods fragile? Perishable?

Post

Small companies operating principally online and manufacturing or supplying small or relatively low-value items will frequently use the post as their main method of shipment for customers both in their domestic market and abroad.

Courier services

Courier services deliver goods door-to-door for a fixed price. The price for shipment to a particular destination will vary depending on things like whether you want same-day collection, whether you want delivery in 24 hours (in Europe) or several days, and whether you want delivery at the destination to take place at the weekend (if necessary). Prices are naturally higher than for postal services. Courier services are ideal for delivering things like emergency spare parts or small valuable items, but most companies would not use them for normal deliveries because of the cost.

Road

Road transport is by far the most common method used for transporting goods – particularly to neighbouring countries or to countries that are linked by an adequate road transport network. Even where a short sea, tunnel or bridge crossing is required, road transport is still the method of choice. Using road transport it is possible to deliver goods door-to-door, either using the same vehicle or with the goods passing through a transport hub.

Rail

In some circumstances, rail transport can be cheaper than other modes of transport, particularly for transporting bulky goods over long distances. There is now also a significant market in intermodal containers carrying non-bulk goods, where the cargo is transferred between trains and other types of transport. Having said that, rail transport is not well suited to small consignments, and generally exporters only use rail when other modes of transport are not suitable or are relatively expensive.

Airfreight

Airfreight is usually the fastest way of transporting goods – particularly between different continents – but it is often also the most expensive. It is the most cost-effective method of transporting high-value low-volume consignments, but is increasingly being used for shipping other goods where the speed of delivery is critical.

Sea freight

Transporting goods by sea may take longer than using other modes of transport, but it can be very cost-effective, particularly if you are shipping large volumes. If you are shipping over long distances, such as from Australia to China or from India to North America, it is the only method available apart from airfreight. Many different types of ship are used to carry different types of cargo, or to transport that cargo in different ways. The main types are container ships, roll-on/roll-off (ro-ro) ferries, general cargo vessels, bulk carriers and tankers. Shipping routes reflect world trade flows. This means that sailings are more frequent and more numerous on routes where trade volumes are largest. The majority of exporters use 'conference lines' for all of their sea freight consignments.*

Groupage or consolidation

Freight forwarders often group together several consignments that have
the same destination. When shipping goods by road, this could mean
them being able to book half a lorry or even a complete lorry. With container
shipments groupage is quite normal, to make sure that where possible
only full containers are shipped. Using groupage or consolidation can
significantly reduce shipping costs.

Dangerous goods

If you are shipping dangerous goods, then there are specific regulations
relating to their shipment. Dangerous goods are classified using the
United Nations classification system and should be marked with their
name, description and UN number.

Using freight forwarders

The role of a freight forwarder is to help exporters (and importers) to
transport their goods. All exporters use freight forwarders, but when
you are starting to export they can be particularly beneficial, because
of their detailed knowledge about shipping to export destinations,
the paperwork requirements and the regulations that need to be
complied with. Freight forwarders can help you by providing specialist
advice, getting the best deal when booking transport on your behalf
and by grouping or consolidating smaller shipments to save time and
money. If you have a consignment of goods to ship from one country
to another, a forwarder will identify and book the best routes, best
mode of transport and specific carriers for you depending on your
requirements.

The main types of freight forwarder would fit into one of the following
categories:

- local;
- regional;
- national with global partners;
- international brand (eg DHL).

In the UK you can find details of freight forwarders on the British International Freight Association (BIFA) website, **www.bifa.org**.

Labelling and packaging of goods

The best way to make sure that your goods arrive in perfect condition is to get your export packaging and labelling right. What is suitable for domestic shipments will almost certainly not be adequate for shipping goods overseas. The correct marking and labelling of your goods is also important as it will help to make sure that they are properly handled while in transit to their final destination.

Export packaging

Export packaging is also sometimes referred to as transport packaging. It is one of the three main types of packaging that may be needed for exported goods:

- *Export packaging* is the outermost layer of packaging and is designed to protect your goods in transit.
- *Outer packaging* is an intermediate layer of packaging that protects the final product packaging.
- *Sales packaging* is the immediate layer of packaging around your goods, which remains in place when the goods reach their end user.

Although we are primarily concerned with the 'outer layer' export packaging, you should consider all of your packaging requirements together since they are interrelated. When packing goods for export you should take the following into consideration:

- You should choose the most appropriate packing materials for the mode of transport that you are using.
- You should find out whether the country of destination has any specific regulations with regard to the packaging of goods that you need to comply with.
- Where possible, consolidate smaller packages into one larger consignment to provide better protection and reduce shipping costs.

- Bear in mind that during shipment other consignments may be stacked on top of yours. Make sure your method of packaging will provide protection if this should happen.
- Secure and protect your goods within the packaging. Heavy goods may need to be bolted to the support. You should also consider using a filling material between the goods and the outer packaging.
- Make sure that you have adequate insurance in place while your goods are being packed. (This is particularly important if you are using an outside company to carry out your export packaging for you.)

Types of export packaging

The materials used in export packaging include wood, metal, plastic, paper and textiles. The main types of packaging in common use are:

- *Cartons*. This is the most widely used type of outer packing.
- *Crates and cases*. Crates used to be made of wood, but this is less common now, because of the high cost of timber and the need to treat with pesticides and to certify for certain markets.
- *Drums*. Metal or plastic drums are commonly used to transport liquids, powders or goods that need to be kept dry.
- *Sacks*. These are available in a range of materials from paper to plastic.
- *Pallets*. These allow smaller packing units such as boxes or cartons to be grouped together.
- *Wrapping*. Shrink wrapping is often used with goods stacked on pallets to add stability and protect the goods.
- *Unpacked*. A wide range of bulk items are shipped 'unpacked'.

Containers

There are a number of internationally recognised container types, including refrigerated units. There are two basic sizes – the 20-foot container with a volume of 33.2 cubic metres, and the 40-foot container with a volume of 67.7 cubic metres. The goods inside will still need packaging, but the container offers protection and increased security from theft. The key advantages of packing goods into containers are:

- It offers multi-modal transport that is very easy to use.
- It gives you the opportunity to offer a door-to-door service.
- Loading and unloading are both quick and efficient.
- Your goods have a high level of security during transit.

Break-bulk

The term 'break-bulk' refers to goods carried as general cargo, rather than in containers. They are usually packed in crates, rather than just being loose, but with this type of shipment there is a greater potential risk of damage during transit.

How to decide what type of export packaging to use

The main purpose of export packaging is to make sure that your goods reach their destination in perfect condition. The export packaging that you use has to protect your goods from damage caused by movement, handling and the elements.

The key factors that should help you to decide which type of packaging to use are the following:

- *The type of goods being shipped.* Factors such as whether the goods are bulky, very heavy, very light, fragile or valuable.
- *Protection.* The main purpose of export packaging is to avoid the risk of damage to your goods.
- *Security.* Goods that are being shipped will frequently be left unattended and you need to make sure that your packaging reduces the risk of your goods being stolen or tampered with.
- *Mode of transport.* In general, packaging for airfreight consignments will be lighter than packaging used for sea freight shipments.

- *Cost.* If you try to save money by using a level of packaging that is not up to the job, you will regret it.
- *Food and perishable goods.* The rules are complicated and you should seek advice from your trade association.
- *Dangerous goods.* There are strict regulations for the packaging and transportation of dangerous goods. The rules vary depending on which mode of transport you are using.
- *Wood packaging.* There are international regulations and standards that apply to the use of wood packaging that have been introduced to control the spread of insect pests and wood diseases. Many exporters may find it easier and more cost-effective to consider using other packaging materials.
- *Waste regulations.* Many countries have waste regulations that favour packaging that can be easily recycled or disposed of.

Labelling

When goods are being shipped abroad every package in the consignment needs to be clearly labelled and identifiable. Regardless of the mode of transport that you are using, your consignment must have the correct shipping marks and numbers in accordance with the International Standards Organisation standard ISO 780 and DIN 55 402.

The complete marking must comprise the following three parts:

- shipping mark;
- information mark;
- handling instructions.

The following details should be provided:

- Shipping mark:
  - identification mark, eg initial letters of receiver or shipper, or of receiver's company name;
  - identification number, eg receiver's order number;
  - total number of items in the complete consignment;
  - the sequential number of the item in the consignment, eg 'Package 5 of 15';

- place and port of destination (not the full address, but check for places elsewhere in the world with the same name, eg Paris, France or Paris, Texas).
- Information mark:
  - The country of origin. Check regulations in the export country. Different countries may require the country of origin to be marked in different ways. For some products the country of origin may also need to be marked on the goods themselves or their individual sales packaging.
  - Details of the weight of the package (in kg).
  - Dimensions of the packages (in cm).
- Handling instructions:
  'Handling marks' help to ensure that greater care is taken with cargo handling and storage. It must be possible to tell from the markings:
  - whether the package is sensitive to heat or moisture;
  - whether it is at risk of breakage;
  - where the top and bottom are;
  - where the centre of gravity is located;
  - where loading tackle may be safely slung.
- Special markings:
  - Marking as per ISPM 15 for containers made from solid wood.
  - Hazardous goods must also be clearly marked.

ISO 780 and DIN 55 402 include details of the internationally recognised handling symbols, including a picture of a wine glass to show that the contents of the package are fragile and arrow symbols to show the correct upright position of the package.

Transport insurance

When shipping your goods abroad you will find that most companies in the chain you use to move your goods operate under conditions that limit their liability in cases of loss, damage or delay. So if you want to have adequate insurance cover, it is prudent to take out your own insurance to ensure that you can claim compensation if there is any financial loss to your business. There are a range of different types of insurance cover available.

General cargo insurance

A typical cargo insurance policy covers goods in transit by road, rail, sea or air. It provides cover against accidental damage and other risks. The cost of the insurance and the circumstances in which you will receive compensation will depend on:

- **the value of goods in transit;**
- **the expiry date of the insurance policy;**
- **whether the journey is domestic (eg to the docks or airport) or international.**

Goods-in-transit insurance

The level of cover that you have will depend on the agreements that you have with your customers or suppliers. They are, however, likely to provide only basic cover and you should consider taking out additional insurance with a third-party broker or via your freight forwarder.

Basic shipping insurance cover (limited liability)

Under a variety of transport modal conventions, you automatically have basic insurance cover when shipping your goods by road, rail, sea or air. But this basic insurance offers you only the minimum of protection for your goods in the event of loss, damage or delay. It is therefore advisable to have additional insurance with a third-party broker or via your freight forwarder.

Shipping insurance is a complex subject and if you are new to exporting it is wise to get advice from contacts that you have in your own industry or from your trade association or local chamber of commerce.

Export documentation

When goods are being shipped overseas they should be accompanied by the correct documentation. If you fail to ensure that all of the documents are correct, you may not get paid on time and your customer may not be able to assume ownership of your goods or services. We can only give a short summary of key documentation here. This is a complex subject and even though most companies will use their freight forwarder to guide them in the preparation and completion of correct export documentation, any company involved in exporting needs to get professional training for its staff on this subject.

When transporting goods within the EU, it is not a legal requirement to carry invoices and despatch notes; packing lists are often used as accompanying documents. But many carriers still demand an invoice to make sure that they will avoid any possible delays at customs. All goods being exported outside the EU must be accompanied by an export declaration and another supporting document, which is usually the invoice.

Export documentation can be divided into four broad categories:

- **transportation;**
- **commercial;**
- **insurance;**
- **payment.**

Transportation documents

There are a number of documents that are commonly used for the movement of goods:

- *Bill of Lading.* **This is used as evidence of the contract between a company and the carrier it is using. It also acts as a certificate of title to the goods and is a fully negotiable document.**
- *Air waybill.* **This is issued by airlines to acknowledge receipt of goods to be transported by airfreight and serves the same purpose for air shipments that the Bill of Lading serves for sea**

shipments. Unlike the Bill of Lading, however, the air waybill is not a document of title to the goods.

- *The CMR note* (Convention des Marchandises par Route). This is, in effect, a 'road waybill' and is a standard contract of carriage that should accompany all consignments of goods that are being transported internationally by road.
- *The CIM note* (Convention Internationale des Marchandises par Chemin de Fer). This is a 'rail waybill' and sets the conditions for the international movement of goods by rail.
- *Standard Shipping Note* (SSN). The SSN is used to accompany deliveries of non-hazardous goods in transit. By using an SSN you can complete the same standard document, regardless of which port, airport or clearance depot the goods are going to.
- *Dangerous Goods Note* (DGN). This is used to accompany hazardous goods in transit to the docks, to a forwarder or to an inland clearance depot.
- *Export Cargo Shipping Instruction* (ECSI). This is the instruction from the exporter to the freight forwarder or carrier.

Commercial documents

The commercial invoice

A commercial invoice should be signed and dated and should contain at least the following information:

- a description of the goods;
- the weight of the goods (in kg);
- the value of the goods;
- the country of origin;
- details of the consignor and consignee.

It can also be useful to include the transport details.

Some countries have particular requirements with regard to the layout of invoices. You can get advice on this from your freight forwarder.

Other common commercial documentation

- *Certificates of origin.* These specify where the goods were manufactured and are often required in countries that have preferential trade agreements in place. They are used to confirm that the goods originate in the exporting country so that the correct customs tariff can be applied to the goods. In North America, a NAFTA certificate of origin is required for goods traded among the NAFTA countries if the goods are NAFTA qualified and the importer is claiming zero-duty preference.
- *Consular invoices.* These are commercial invoices that need to be certified by a consular representative of the country to which the goods are being exported.
- *ATA carnet.* Certain types of goods that are temporarily exported can avoid all customs controls and charges by the use of an ATA carnet.

Insurance documents

For shipments to certain markets you may need to provide copies of insurance documents:

- insurance policy;
- certificate of insurance, which provides documentary evidence that the cargo is insured.

Finance and payment documents

- *Bills of exchange* (sometimes called 'cash against documents') are used for documentary collection.
- *Letters of credit.* This is the most popular method of guaranteeing payment for international transactions, particularly when shipping to less creditworthy countries.

Classifying your goods

If you trade internationally, it is essential that your goods are classified so that you can identify what duties and controls apply and ensure a correct customs declaration. Classifying your goods correctly will ensure that you pay the right duty and that you know whether an export licence is required. You have a legal responsibility to ensure that the correct classification is applied, whether or not you have an agent who handles customs entries on your behalf. Incorrect classification can lead to delays in clearing goods, overpayment of duties and possible penalties. As well as being used in import and export declarations, the classification of commodities is used to collect data and trade statistics.

The Harmonised Commodity Description and Coding System (HS)

The Harmonised Commodity Description and Coding System, generally referred to as 'Harmonised System' or simply 'HS', is a multi-purpose international product nomenclature developed by the World Customs Organisation (WCO), **www.wcoomd.org**. The HS, also often known as 'tariff numbers', is the coding system used for trade worldwide.

It comprises about 5,000 commodity groups, each identified by a six-digit code, arranged in a legal and logical structure and supported by well-defined rules to achieve uniform classification. The system is used by more than 200 countries and economies as a basis for their customs tariffs and for the collection of international trade statistics. Most of these countries set up their own national customs tariff, based on the HS system. Over 98 per cent of the merchandise in international trade is classified in terms of the HS.

The major complication with HS codes is that only the first six digits of the classification number are uniform among countries that use the system. The first two digits are known as the HS chapter, the second two are known as the HS heading and the third two comprise the HS subheading. Most countries add a few further digits to classify the product in more detail, but these first six digits cannot be changed. To export your product you need to know the complete product classification code for your own country, and also the complete classification code for the country that you are exporting to.

The European Union (EU)

EU countries classify goods for import or export according to the Tariff. This is a system of 'Commodity Codes' that are used across the EU based on the EU TARIC (TARif Intégré Communautaire). Each community country has its own version, and in the UK the classification is carried out using 'The Integrated Tarif of the United Kingdom' (The Tariff). Working out the code is complicated, but UK exporters can get assistance on the Business Link website, **www.businesslink.gov.uk**, by using the free online tool 'UK Trade Tariff' to find the correct trade tariff for their products. A similar service is also available by telephone from HM Revenue & Customs on its Tariff Classification Service Enquiry line on 01702 366 077.

The United States

The United States uses 10-digit codes to classify all products and commodities. As with other international classification systems, the first six digits are the HS number. The last four digits are unique to the United States and classify the product in greater detail. This complete 10-digit code is known as a Schedule B code. All Schedule B codes are contained in the book *The Schedule B: Statistical classification of domestic and foreign commodities exported from the United States*. Schedule B codes are administered by the US Census Bureau and the book is available on its website, **www.census.gov**. The whole book can be viewed on the website or purchased through the Government Printing Office (GPO), **http://bookstore.gpo.gov**.

On the US Census website under 'Schedule B Validation', you can type in your 10-digit number and it will check that it is valid and tell you the relevant product description. If you need further help you can consult a commodity specialist at the US Census Bureau Foreign Trade Division on (301) 763–3259 (durable goods), (301) 763 3484 (non durable goods) or contact your local Export Assistance Center.

Reporting procedures

Governments collect trade statistics and details of exports from and imports into their countries. The rules and regulations vary from country to country, but in most countries exporters have a legal obligation to provide details of their exports, including the tariff commodity codes and values. This information is often collected by tax or customs authorities on either export documentation or tax returns, such as those for Value Added Tax (VAT) in the European Union.

Reporting procedures for exporters from EU member states

The situation for EU member states is complicated by the fact that importers and exporters have to make separate declarations of transactions with other EU states and transactions with countries outside the EU. The reporting procedures vary depending on the country that the goods are being shipped to:

- **exports to other EU countries: Intrastat return;**
- **exports to EFTA countries: SAD;**
- **exports to the rest of the world: SAD.**

The Single Administrative Document (SAD) was introduced in 1988 to replace over 150 customs documents in use at that time within both the EU and EFTA. In 1993 the EU itself moved over to Intrastat for reporting within the EU, but the SAD is still used for making export, transit and import declarations for shipments to EFTA countries and to all other countries outside the EU. In the UK the SAD is also referred to as form C88.

Guidance on the reporting process and on submitting export declarations can be obtained from HM Revenue and Customs, either on its website, **www.hmrc.gov.uk**, or by phone. Support material is also available on the Business Link website, **www.businesslink.gov.uk**.

Reporting procedures for US exporters

US exporters have to complete a Shipper's Export Declaration (SED) where the value of the commodities being shipped, classified under any single Schedule B number, exceeds $2,500. The SED is used to control exports and is a source document for official US statistics. SEDs must be prepared and submitted for all shipments (regardless of value) that require an export licence or are destined for countries restricted by the Export Administration regulations. The US Census Bureau's Foreign Trade Division controls the SED. In 2008 the bureau made electronic filing of the SED mandatory using AESDirect. AESDirect is a web-based application that allows an SED to be filed electronically. Information is available on the website, **www.aesdirect.gov**.

*   Many shipping companies operating on the same sea route join together into 'freight conferences'. They co-operate on both rates and schedules and usually offer customers a discount if they use only 'conference line' vessels. Although conference lines do not compete on rates, they do virtually guarantee the exporter a regular service, with a ship departing to a particular destination every week or every two weeks, for example.

11

Managing the risks

The pattern of export trade that your company develops will be defined in large part by the type of business that it is and the type of product that you sell. When risk management companies are offering advice and insurance services to exporters, they will usually define the company's way of doing business as one of the following:

- occasional exporters;
- new exporters;
- companies supplying goods to overseas markets and to specific customers on a regular basis;
- companies supplying large 'one-off' sales contracts;
- companies supplying capital or semi-capital goods for major overseas projects;
- companies providing services.

Understanding the market

When dealing with overseas markets you need to understand the differences that exist in different cultures and different parts of the world. In most overseas markets, you will be dealing with a different language, a different business culture and probably also a different legal system. All of these can create problems. You can reduce the risks by researching the market thoroughly, getting advice where necessary and by either employing someone who speaks the local language or making sure that your distributor or agent has staff that you can deal with who speak your language.

Country risks

The country that you are dealing with may in itself present certain risks. It may be economically weak or politically unstable. The key things that you need to consider are outlined below.

Political
- changes in government that may affect trading policy or delay the transfer of payment for goods;
- the imposition of import restrictions, after your contract is signed, that prevent you from shipping the goods (which you may have already part-manufactured);
- the imposition of embargoes, tariffs or other quotas;
- internal or external threats to the country, including war or civil unrest.

Economic
- the willingness or ability of the government and government agencies to pay their debts;
- the competence and stability of the banking system (collapses of the banking system are not uncommon in the developing world);
- the availability of trade finance for exports to a particular country;
- the ability of the private sector to pay for its imports;
- lack of foreign exchange reserves;
- the inconvertibility of local currencies;
- the imposition of exchange controls that prevent the transfer of funds.

Climate is also a risk factor. Some regions of the world regularly experience natural disasters such as flooding, hurricanes, droughts or earthquakes. When these occur there may be major disruption of day-to-day business for the private sector and the government.

Customer risks

You should always check the creditworthiness of your customer. This type of information can be obtained by running a credit check though a reputable credit agency such as Dun & Bradstreet. Ideally you need to know the following:

- **The identity of the customer. Do they have a legally established business in their country?**
- **Does the person you are dealing with have the legal authority to act for the company?**
- **The credit rating of the customer. Even in low-risk countries such as those in the EU or the United States, customers can still pose a credit risk to you.**
- **Is the customer solvent and likely to remain so?**
- **What is the usual period of credit offered in your customer's country?**
- **The trading history of your customer. Is its payment record consistent?**
- **Do your products fit with the business profile of your customer?**
- **Will your customer be able to pay its bill? (You can take out export credit insurance, even for low-risk countries.)**

Creditworthiness

Once you have checked and confirmed that your customer or distributor is solvent, you need to decide how you want to trade. Do you want to offer credit or do you feel that you need to get paid for your goods before they are shipped?

When you start to offer credit to export customers, you need to decide how much credit you are prepared to advance. Before you do this you need to consider:

- How much credit do you already have on your trading accounts, including credit outstanding in your domestic market?
- How much do you know about your customer/distributor and its trading/payment record?
- What is the absolute maximum amount of credit that you will extend to this customer?
- What would be the impact on your business if the customer delays payment or does not pay at all?
- Remember that payment terms for exporting are usually longer than in domestic markets – 30 days' payment terms at home often become 60 days or even more with export business.
- Can you finance the credit you will need to offer, and if so, how will you finance it?

Financing credit and the risks involved is one of the most difficult problems facing would-be exporters. Steady growth in your export business is better than taking risks with credit to achieve rapid growth. As a rule of thumb, your export business will cost you roughly twice as much to finance in credit terms as your domestic business.

In setting a credit limit for a regular customer or distributor, you need to take into account how much business you have on your books for that customer and not just how much debt is outstanding.

The risks of currency and foreign exchange

If you develop a significant export business, foreign currencies and the fluctuations of the foreign exchange market are certain to impact on it. If you sell goods in your own currency, you know what your margins are and how much profit you can make from a certain level of business. If you sell in a foreign currency, fluctuations in exchange rates can significantly affect your margins and profits. So you need to protect yourself against foreign exchange risk.

Buying and selling foreign currency

There are a number of ways to buy or sell foreign currency:

- *Spot dealing.* If you buy or sell currency on the 'spot' market, the exchange rate will be the rate at that point in time. Spot dealing is the simplest way for you to buy or sell foreign currency, but the risk is that you have no way of knowing what the rate will be until the transaction is carried out and the spot rate that you receive will be set by the market conditions at the time.
- *Forward contracts.* Forward contracts are available for any period up to two years and if you take one out you know exactly how much you will get paid in your own currency when your customer makes his payment to you.
- *Currency options.* A currency option is similar to a forward contract, but as well as protecting you from adverse exchange rate movements it will also allow you to make gains if the market moves in your favour.
- *Foreign currency bank account.* Your company can also open a foreign currency bank account. This is particularly useful if you have both expenses and revenues in one particular currency as you can use income in that currency to pay expenditure and minimise the need to actually exchange currencies.

There are three ways that you can deal with foreign exchange risks:

- *Do nothing.* This is a high-risk option. It means that as and when you need to convert foreign currency back into your own currency, you will be dealing with the spot market. If you do this, it will be impossible to properly plan and budget for your export business.
- *Manage the effect of currency fluctuations yourself.* This is a better option. If you do this, you will at least be able to calculate what your possible risks may be and to take action accordingly.
- *Take out foreign exchange contracts.* This is the safest way to manage the risks. This allows you to fix the exchange rate so that you know exactly how much you will receive in your own currency, when your invoice is paid.

Managing the effect of currency fluctuations yourself

If your company is based in the European Union, the United States or any other country with a stable and easily convertible currency, you can initially decide only to sell in your own currency. In doing so you are transferring the foreign exchange risk to your customers. Major customers may not be prepared to take this currency risk and may prefer to deal with your competitors if they are prepared to sell in the local currency. So an alternative is to produce a price list in a currency that is the currency of your major customers. Apart from your own currency, it is really only sensible to consider having a price list in a major traded currency, such as the US dollar, the euro or the pound sterling.

Even if you only transact a small part of your business in foreign currencies, you need to understand its potential impact on your margins and profits. If you are selling goods from a foreign currency price list, a 10 per cent change in the exchange rate between that currency and your own will decrease or increase your selling price in your own currency by 10 per cent. But that will have a far greater impact on your margins. If you have a gross margin of 40 per cent on sales in the foreign currency, a 10 per cent reduction in the exchange rate will take away 25 per cent of that margin. Equally, an increase of 10 per cent in the value of the currency will increase your margin by 25 per cent.

Any company involved in exporting will set expected exchange rates for the key foreign currencies used for its overseas sales when it set its annual budget. If the value of your overseas sales in foreign currencies is significant, you need to manage the risks professionally.

Taking out forward foreign exchange contracts

The safest way to deal with exchange rate risk is to use forward foreign exchange contracts. You can contract to buy or sell a fixed amount of one currency into another currency at a particular point in time at an exchange rate that is fixed when you take out the contract. This way you know at the outset exactly how much you will be paid for the goods in your own currency.

Forward exchange rate contracts can only protect your business for a limited period of time. They can be used to protect you from risks during the period from when you take an order to when you are paid for it. They cannot protect your margins from long-term currency fluctuations.

If you consider the US$/UK£ exchange rate over the last 20 years, it has varied from between very nearly $1:£1 to as much as $2.4:£1, but for most of the time it has probably been in the range of $1.4 to $1.8:£1. Major fluctuations have also occurred between the US$ and the euro and the Japanese yen. In the short term you can protect your margin by taking out forward foreign exchange contracts, but in the long term you have to decide if your company can accept the reduced margin, while you try to cut costs and also hope that the exchange rate will eventually move the other way.

Delivery delays and frustrated exports

When accepting large individual export orders or contracts, it is wise to try to get payment terms that include a significant down-payment with the order. If you are supplying capital or semi-capital goods for major projects, it is not uncommon to find that the customer's timescale has changed and that they would prefer to take the goods later. This can cause you significant financial costs if you have already commenced manufacture and are going to be unable to ship the goods when scheduled. Even worse is what is called a 'frustrated export'. This is when the customer refuses the goods or attempts to cancel the order at an advanced point in the manufacturing schedule. Your export strategy should include a plan to either resell the goods to another market, modify the goods for resale, reuse components or parts in other contracts or realise a salvage value for the goods.

Intellectual property rights in international trade

Your intellectual property is the sum of the unique ideas, products and information that add commercial value to your business. It can be a brand, the name of your business, an invention, a design or some type of artistic or written material that you create. Intellectual property includes copyrights, patents, trademarks and logos, but also extends to plants and seeds with national or variety rights, and goods that infringe designations of origin or geographical indications. Intellectual property rights (IPR) give legal protection to your intellectual property, preventing others from profiting from it commercially. If you are not sure what you have in the way of intellectual property that could or should be protected, you can find out about intellectual property on the Intellectual Property Office website, **www.ipo.gov.uk**.

There are four main types of IP rights that can be used to protect inventions or creations. These are:

- *Patents*. **Patents protect rights to devices that make things work.**
- *Trademarks*. **Trademarks are signs (like words and logos) that distinguish goods and services in the marketplace.**
- *Designs*. **Design rights protect the appearance of a product/logo.**
- *Copyright*. **Copyright is an automatic right that applies when the work is fixed, written or recorded in some way.**

In protecting your IP rights you need to make sure that you protect them both in your domestic market and overseas. You need to make sure that you have cover in place in all of the markets that you are in or may want to export to in the future. Although copyright is an automatic right that applies worldwide, other intellectual property rights are not so comprehensive and may be non-existent unless you apply for and receive cover. Once you start exporting your products, you also need to consider how you can protect your IP from being copied or stolen in countries where IP protection is less comprehensive than in the major economies.

Avoiding litigation

When selling to a number of countries, including the United States, you also need to check your product literature to reduce product liability risks. Customers in the US are statistically much more likely to take legal action if your literature fails to warn of potential harm that could result from the misuse of your product.

Personal and company risk

There are unfortunately still many countries in the world where the risks of exporting are not just limited to financial aspects. Crime, both organised and localised, terrorism, bribery and corruption can all be very real risks to companies and to company personnel involved in exporting. UK Trade & Investment's Overseas Security Information for Business (OSIB) provides UK companies with information relating to the security-related risks that companies face when doing business overseas. They provide information about security-related issues under the following headings:

- **political and economic;**
- **bribery and corruption;**
- **terrorism threats;**
- **protective security advice;**
- **intellectual property;**
- **organised crime.**

The UKTI website, **www.ukti.gov.uk**, gives up to date OSIB information for more than 90 different countries. You should not underestimate the personal risks that you run if you ignore sensible security advice.

Bribery and corruption are also major risks in some countries. You may be sure in your own mind that you would never get involved in such activities, but remember that bribery works in two directions and you may find that you are offered bribes and put under significant pressure (or threat) when you turn them down.

Risk management and insurance services

So should you manage all of the risks of exporting yourself or should you use the services of a credit management and insurance provider? In many ways this would depend on the type and range of your export business, the expertise that you have in-house and the attitude of top management.

There are two extremes: if you have a limited amount of export business that you are developing and most of your sales are through distributors whom you have been working with for some time, then you can probably handle all of the risk management yourself. If you supply items of capital equipment for major long-term projects that take several years to complete and your customers are mainly in developing countries, then you probably need to take out credit insurance such as Export Credits Guarantee Department (ECGD) cover for every contract.

In my experience, if you have a competent credit management team in-house and managing the risks is company policy agreed by top management, then you can handle most of the risks of day-to-day business yourself, but should still take out export insurance for large 'one-off' orders or contracts. But if your top management does not want to take any risks as you develop your export business and your margins are sufficient to cover the additional costs of a credit insurance policy, you should take one out.

If you decide to manage the risks yourself you need to have a team that will usually consist of senior personnel from your sales, finance and logistics departments. These personnel need to have the expertise and resources to:

- **research the country and associated risks;**
- **gather credit and background information about existing and potential customers and distributors;**
- **decide when and where you need to rely on credit insurance;**
- **select the most appropriate and cost-effective policy;**
- **manage the credit insurance policy to get the best out of it.**

Insurance products and services

The insurance product that you will select will depend on your type of business, but the following are the main products that are available:

- **An arrangement with a credit insurer to analyse your existing business, consider your future plans and cover the risks on your exports. The service can be set up to cover all of your export sales** or just large or key accounts. It can also be limited to specific products or individual geographic areas.

- A 'one-off' policy for a particular contract.
- A managed credit insurance scheme. This type of arrangement is particularly suited to small exporters or companies new to exporting.

The major credit insurance companies have a long experience and understanding of the risks involved in international trade. They provide a professional approach to export risk management. By covering your commercial debts and making sure that you get paid even if your customer fails to pay, they help to provide your export sales team with the confidence that they need to maximise your export sales growth.

Useful websites

Support for exporters – UK

www.ukti.gov.uk – government organisation providing support for exporters, including market reports, country reports and support for exhibitions, trade missions, etc.

www.businesslink.gov.uk – the government's online resource for businesses. The site includes support material for exporters.

www.export.org.uk – The Institute of Export – the UK Centre of Exporting Excellence.

www.bis.gov.uk – Department for Business Innovation & Skills (BIS).

www.britishchambers.org.uk /zones /export – British Chambers of Commerce export information.

www.sitpro.org.uk – archived website of SITPRO, the UK trade facilitation agency.

Government support for exporters – other countries

www.export.gov – US Department of Commerce. The US government's main online resource for US exporters.

www.buyusa.gov – US Commercial Service overseas websites.

www.austrade.gov.au – The Australia Trade Commission providing support to Australian exporters.

www.tfocanada.ca – The Trade Facilitation Office. Canadian export support.

http://english.ccpit.org – The China Council for the Promotion of International Trade supports Chinese exporters.

www.cbbc.org – The China–Britain Business Council.

www.indiatradefair.com – India Trade Promotion Agency (ITPO) is the key government agency supporting Indian exporters.

www.ukibc.com – The UK India Business Council.

www.thedti.gov.za – Government agency supporting South African exporters.

www.nzte.govt.nz – New Zealand Trade and Enterprise supporting New Zealand exporters.

www.jetro.go.jp – information on doing business in Japan.

www.gtai.de – Trade and Invest. German export support.

www.exporter.gouv.fr – French government support for exporters.

www.ice.gov.it – Istituto Nazionale per il Commercio Estero. Italian government support for exporters.

Other useful sites for exporters

www.wto.org – World Trade Organisation.

www.worldchambers.com – World Chambers Network, which is the official global portal of Chambers of Commerce.

www.iccwbo.org – International Chamber of Commerce.

www.wcoomd.org – World Customs Organisation.

www.iccbookshop.com – ICC United Kingdom Bookshop, supplier of information on Incoterms.

www.europa.eu – European Union website.

www.census.gov – US Census Bureau administers Schedule B codes.

www.bifa.org – British International Freight Association.

www.abi.org.uk – The Association of British Insurers.

www.biba.org.uk – The British Insurance Brokers Association (BIBA).

www.tis-gdv.de – transport information service of the German Insurance Association.

www.exportuk.co.uk – UK Exporters Ltd – publishers of *British Exporters* CD. Offer international press release service, agent finder service and membership of British Exporters Club.

Government statistics

www.ons.gov.uk – Office for National Statistics – government statistics including economy, regional trends, consumer trends and Product Sales Reports (PRODCOM information).

http://epp.eurostat.ec.europa.eu – Eurostat – provider of European statistics.

www.thestationeryoffice.com – largest supplier of official publications, both online and with various branches around the UK.

Financial data

www.dnb.co.uk – Dun & Bradstreet – financial information on companies.

Market and sector reports

www.ukti.gov.uk.

www.export.gov.

www.euromonitor.com.

www.frost.com – Frost & Sullivan.

www.keynote.co.uk.

www.eiu.com – Economist Intelligence Unit – country reports.

Market research organisations

www.marketresearch.org.uk – The Market Research Society.

www.esomar.org – Esomar (European Society for Opinion and Market Research).

www.britishchambers.org.uk/emrs – government export marketing research scheme.

Trade associations

www.taforum.org – Trade Association Forum – find trade associations in your industry.

Trade and specialised directories

www.kompass.co.uk.
www.kellysearch.com.
www.yell.com – Yellow Pages.
www.nridigital.com – information on industries and projects.

Internet

www.nominet.org.uk – holder of UK domain names.
www.hostingreview.com – reviews of web hosting companies.

Distribution law

www.kemplittle.com – law firm specialising in distribution and agency law.

Intellectual property

www.ipo.gov.uk – The Intellectual Property Office – patents, trademarks, copyright.
www.uspto.gov – US Patent and Trademark Office.

Other general sources

www.oecd.org – Organisation of Economic Cooperation and Development – GDP data and a wide range of statistics for OECD members.
www.eiu.com – Economist Intelligence Unit.
www.kompass.com – the business-to-business search engine.
www.worldatlas.com – worldwide country information.
www.wikipedia.org – free online encyclopedia.
www.cia.gov – CIA website. Publishes *World Factbook*.

Types of government support services available

To show how extensive and helpful the tools and services offered by government organisations can be, this section provides an outline of the services available to UK exporters from UK Trade & Investment (UKTI). Similar support services are available to exporters in many countries from their local government support agencies, so wherever your business is based, this information should be useful in showing you what opportunities to look out for.

Example: Government support available to exporters in the UK

The UKTI website, **www.ukti.gov.uk**, and the Business Link website, **www.businesslink.gov.uk**, provide the online interface for UK companies seeking export support. A vast array of information on exporting and export markets is available. Although both sites cover a lot of the same subjects, the material and guides that you can download from the UKTI site are more related to export markets, market sectors, help in entering specific markets, making overseas visits, taking part in overseas exhibitions, trade missions and so on. The Business Link site has much more information on the 'nuts and bolts' of shipping your goods abroad. They have a wealth of information on things like export documentation requirements, customs regulations, VAT requirements, export insurance and the like.

UKTI provide a number of interactive assessment tools on their website, including a questionnaire that will help you recognise your strengths and isolate your weaknesses as you get ready to break into export markets. There is also a tool to allow you to identify export opportunities in any chosen market.

How to start using the service

If you enter your postcode on the UKTI website it will bring up the name, contact telephone number and e-mail address of your nearest international trade adviser. (Your Local Enterprise Partnership or Chamber of Commerce can also refer you.) You can then contact this adviser for specific information and guidance.

UKTI's international trade advisers can provide you with professional advice on their range of services, including financial subsidies, export documentation, contacts in overseas markets, overseas visits, e-commerce, export training and market research. Support is available for companies of all sizes and with all levels of export experience, but schemes that offer financial support or grants are normally restricted to what UKTI defines as small and medium-sized enterprises (SMEs).

Virtually all UKTI programmes are personalised and specifically adapted to the requirements of individual businesses. Your international trade adviser will identify whether your company is new to exporting (in which case UKTI will offer a set of services including 'Passport to Export') or is an experienced exporter (in which case they will offer services including 'Gateway to Global Growth').

Individual services offered by UKTI

I will cover the main services below, but I would mention that programmes on offer may vary and may be changed from time to time, and the financial support offered may be increased or cut, depending on changes in government spending. Also, new web pages will be added and some will be withdrawn. Nevertheless, having used the services for many years, I can assure you that the general trend has been to continually improve the service available and if financial support is withdrawn from one area, it is usually soon reintroduced in another.

Passport to Export

Passport to Export is a skills-based programme that provides new and inexperienced exporters with the training, planning and ongoing support that they need to succeed overseas. It offers a business health-check, mentoring from one of its local export professionals, an individual export plan and a range of developmental training from which to choose.

Export Marketing Research Scheme (EMRS)

This is a subsidised service that the British Chambers of Commerce administer on behalf of UKTI. It helps companies carry out export marketing research on all major aspects of any export venture. This can include:

- **market size and segmentation;**
- **regulations and legislation;**
- **customer needs, usage and attitudes;**
- **distribution channels;**
- **trends;**
- **competitor activity, strategy and performance.**

Overseas Market Introduction Service (OMIS)

OMIS is a service whereby, for a competitive fee, you can commission research into a particular market. This can include preparation of a list of potential distributors in the country and even help in setting up meetings with them. OMIS uses the services of the UKTI trade teams located in the British embassies, high commissions and consulates across the world.

Tradeshow Access Programme

The Tradeshow Access Programme provides support for participants in overseas exhibitions and seminars. Participation is usually as part of a group, which is a big advantage for inexperienced businesses. The group is often on a UK stand, which is split into individual sub-stands for the participating companies. Grants are available to help SMEs with the cost of overseas exhibitions that are supported by the programme.

Sector-focused missions

Sector-focused trade missions last between three and eight days. Small businesses taking part in these trade missions are eligible for travel grants to cover up to half the cost of the visit. The missions are often specific to a particular industry or event. The process works in a similar way to exhibition support and is often managed by a Chamber of Commerce. Missions are an ideal way to visit a market that you are unfamiliar with, and you can gain from the experience of the UKTI mission leader and others on the mission as well as from the local contacts that you make.

Other services for experienced exporters

Some of the services mentioned above, such as the Overseas Market Introduction Service and the Export Marketing Research Scheme, are used by experienced exporters as much as by newcomers. But there are some additional services that are specifically aimed at helping experienced exporters to grow their business.

Gateway to Global Growth

This is UKTI's flagship package for experienced exporters. It is a free service that offers companies a strategic review, planning and support to help them grow their business overseas. The solutions suggested could be complex; in some cases they may require services offered by other public and private sector companies as well as specific services offered by UKTI.

Overseas Market Introduction Service (OMIS)

This service will be extended with two new services for experienced exporters that will be piloted in 2012: Global OMIS to provide longer-term support for larger companies that want to use UKTI services around the world to secure multiple orders; and a bespoke service (linked to a success fee for UKTI) to help companies to win major trade contracts using dedicated UKTI and external specialist resources.

Export Communications Review (ECR)

This service is offered by the British Chambers of Commerce to provide companies with impartial and objective advice on language and cultural issues to help them to develop an effective communications strategy to improve their competitiveness in their existing and future export markets. It offers companies an on-site review of the way that they currently communicate with their export markets. Typically, this would include a review of the company's website and written materials, and could also include meetings with the company's customers and agents/distributors. The reviews are carried out by accredited export communications consultants who have been trained in export communications by the British Chambers of Commerce.

The Business Opportunities Service

The Business Opportunities Service is a free service providing sales leads that come via UKTI's global contacts network. Over 400 Business Opportunities are published each month. These may come from any industry sector in over 100 overseas markets. The leads range from market pointers to private sector opportunities, multilateral aid agency tenders to public sector leads. Any UK company can register for this service on the UKTI website. When you receive a lead that is of interest, you can ask UKTI for more specific information and you will also be sent the contact details for the company.

High-value Opportunities Programme

Very large-scale, high-value international projects and contracts offer enormous opportunities for businesses of all sizes. This programme offers intensive 'high level' support for larger companies seeking overseas contracts ranging in value from £250 million to £1 billion, with supply chain opportunities for SMEs.

Partnership with ECGD

UKTI and ECGD will work together to promote the Export Enterprise Finance Guarantee (ExEFG) to SMEs. This provides guarantees to lenders who facilitate the provision of short-term export finance lines of up to £1 million to exporting SMEs. Other products include a Bond Support Scheme to help exporters to raise tender and contract bonds, an Export Working Capital Scheme to facilitate access to working capital for specific export contracts, and a Foreign Exchange Credit Support Scheme to help exporters manage their exposure to foreign exchange rate movements.

Other services

Online peer self-help

UKTI is developing an online network of UK companies, so that they can support each other and share knowledge in order to internationalise their business. The online content will include financial, sector and market data, as well as information based on the practical experience and wisdom of users. This service will be rolled out during the course of 2012.

Social media

The UKTI website, **www.ukti.gov.uk**, was revamped in 2010 and is now state of the art with improved functionality and navigation. There are integrated social media feeds to the UKTI blog (with RSS to send you updates by e-mail), Twitter – UKTI had over 9,200 followers in April 2011 (if you join they will send you short, timely messages) – Flickr (showing the UKTI photostream), YouTube (the UKTIWeb's channel with a wide variety of material including sectoral showcases and opportunities in specific markets) and LinkedIn (you can join the UKTI group, which had over 6,700 members in May 2011).

Springboard magazine

UKTI publishes a magazine, *Springboard*, six times a year. This is free and you can subscribe by calling 0800 298 3880 or by visiting **http://springboard.managemyaccount.co.uk**. *Springboard* includes news and updates on UKTI initiatives, features on export success stories, interviews with successful exporters and entrepreneurs, country focus articles and a directory of events.